SINGLE,

SAVED, &

SEEKING

HIM

SINGLE, SAVED, & SEEKING HIM

ENCOURAGEMENT FOR THE SINGLE CHRISTIAN

Amina R. Maybank

Words From Heaven Publishing

Printed in the United States of America

ISBN 978-0-692-25613-8

Words From Heaven Publishing
P.O. Box 44473
Philadelphia, PA 19144

www.wfhpublishing.com

For those who feel forgotten...
Can a woman forget her nursing child
And have no compassion on the son of her
womb?
Even these may forget, but I will not forget you.
Behold, I have inscribed you on the palms of My
hands;
Your walls are continually before Me.

Isaiah 49:15-16

TABLE OF CONTENTS

ACKNOWLEDGEMENTS

To My Lord & Savior Jesus Christ, I'm so grateful for the plans that You have for me. I'm grateful that you were always there, even at my worst times. When I wanted to walk away, you wouldn't let me. Thank you for blessing me with the words to write for this book. Thank you for the experiences, and allowing me to use them to minister life to your people. You have given me purpose. I love You.

My mother, Jacquelyn, you're the strongest woman I know. After everything that God has allowed you to endure, you're still here...laughing, joking, and smiling. Thank you for your prayers, encouraging words, and for believing God on my behalf. Thank you for not only being my mother, but for being my friend. I love you always.

My brothers Na'im and Tafarod, thank you for your support and for loving me unconditionally. My sister Quanesha, although you're 10 years younger, I glean so much from you. Your maturity, wisdom, and walk with God encourage me to persevere and above all

1

things—to laugh. You all are my best friends. I love you guys.

Bishop Earl and Prophetess Maria Palmer: my pastors, my teachers, and my spiritual parents...thank you for your sacrifices, prayers, encouraging words, and for uncompromisingly teaching the Word of God. I thank God for you both.

A special thank you to everyone who participated in the creation of this book. May God bless you richly for your generosity.

Be Blessed.

PREFACE

Many singles in the Body of Christ are waiting on God for a spouse. Unfortunately, many have been waiting years and feel like giving up. Some have already given up and gone their own way. Then there are those who truly love God but are not living in obedience to the Word of God. Some are embarrassed to discuss the many feelings and trials that they go through as single adults. As I questioned God about my own circumstances, He revealed to me that I was and am not alone. 1 Peter 5:9 tells us to be steadfast in the faith, knowing that the same sufferings are experienced by our brotherhood in the world. You need to know that you are not alone in the way you feel or in your daily struggles. You need to know that God has not forgotten you. He is right there with you.

God is a God of purpose. Everything He does or does not do is on purpose. As I wrestled with my single status, the Lord showed me that there is purpose in this season of my life. The Bible says, to everything *there is* a season, a time for every *purpose* under Heaven (Ecclesiastes 3:1). With that in mind, I asked God, "What do you want from me in this season?" I realized that if God is who He proclaims, and if He wanted me married, then I would be married. I knew that it was something that I was supposed to birth in this season of my life. Therefore, instead of continuing to manipulate people and circumstances to avoid singleness, I surrendered and sought God. As I sought God, I also struggled with many issues as a single Christian. However, deep down I knew that I was not the only one experiencing these issues. I also knew that I was not experiencing these things in vain. I wanted to do something. I wanted to help my brothers and sisters who were also waiting on God to send them a spouse. In addition, regardless of how I felt about being single, I knew that God wanted me single for such a time as this.

THE GOAL OF THIS BOOK

Honestly, I was afraid to write this book. I didn't want to expose myself. I didn't want to expose the different spirits that I wrestled with daily. I didn't want to become naked and vulnerable before anyone except God. However, I know that my vulnerability will help someone else in the Body of Christ. I can remember the Lord asking me numerous times throughout the years, "How can you write about something that you have not experienced? How can you help

4

people if you don't know how they feel?" Therefore, I prayerfully wrote this book with the intent to encourage, enlighten, and empower every single Christian that reads these words.

As you read this book, I pray that God's Spirit will minister to you in a profound way. May the words that you read challenge and encourage you to become greater in this season of your life. I pray that you will be persuaded to wait on the Lord and stay in the will of God. Know that God loves you. For the LORD God *is* a sun and shield; The LORD will give grace and glory; No good *thing* will He withhold from those who walk uprightly (Psalm 84:11).

INTRODUCTION

INTRODUCTION

I've truly experienced every chapter of this book. I can remember the Lord providing me with chapter titles before I actually experienced them. I knew it wouldn't be long before I had to confront that particular issue, and I knew I would have to confront it before I could write about it. Nevertheless, I went through knowing that my experiences would help other people.

Within the chapters are revelations that the Lord has given me about the different issues that we go through as single Christians. Some of those chapters include, *Surrender*, *God's Timing*, and *Learning Contentment*, among others. The Lord has shown me in His Word, numerous scriptures that single Christians can and should apply to their lives. There are some chapters that I would have rather left out in order to "save face." However, I'm not ashamed of what God has allowed me to endure. I know that my words will be a blessing to you as you read them.

As you read these chapters, read them prayerfully and be honest with yourself. Then ask God to minister to you about these different issues that you are experiencing. I'm convinced that as you read, you will receive revelation, healing, deliverance, and encouragement from these chapters. Feel free to read the chapters that you are drawn to first. You don't need to read this book in any particular order. Take notes on the scriptures that resonate with you and write them down; in them is your deliverance. Ask the Lord to show you how to apply the scriptures to your daily life.

Please know that you're not reading this book by chance. As the Lord ministered to me, He wanted me to share everything He gave me with you. Be encouraged as you continue to wait on the Lord and seek Him.

1

SURRENDER

1

SURRENDER

Father, if you are willing, take this cup from me;
yet not my will, but yours be done.

Luke 22:42

The word surrender means to give in or to hand over. It also means to yield or to submit. How can we, who want to be married, submit ourselves to our spouses if we can't submit ourselves to Christ? Surrendering is saying, "Lord not my will, but your will be done." We need to surrender our desires, our disappointments, our expectations, and our timetables to the Lord. We often say "Lord, your will be done" but fight Him when His will is contrary to our own.

Surrendering your desire for marriage to God doesn't mean you must give up on that desire. It simply means you must place that desire in His hands and trust Him with it, despite the discomfort. Many times in our Christian walk we will have to surrender our will for God's will. We can choose to be angry, bitter, and complain. In the end, we are only hurting ourselves because we are stifling the process of what God wants to accomplish through us.

For a while I wasn't dating anyone. I was going to church and doing all that I knew to be "right." I thought I was surrendered. I was doing all the "right" things, but my heart was not surrendered. I hadn't given the Lord my desire for marriage. I couldn't relinquish it, for some reason. I held on to the desire so tightly. I couldn't even sleep at night because the fact that I was still single with no prospects bothered me that much. The question "Will I ever have children?" tortured me every other day. I was not at rest. I had no peace. I was not surrendered. I'd allowed those torturing spirits to taunt me because I wouldn't enter into God's rest. I would not surrender.

The word surrender may sound negative to some people. It may sound as if you are giving up. In reality, you are exercising your faith. We, as human beings, naturally want to do everything ourselves. We want to make things happen. The idea of handing over your desires to God can seem a bit daunting. However, God often reminds me that He can do a better job at making things happen than I can. In Jeremiah 10:23, the prophet prayed, "I know, O Lord, that the way of man is not in himself, that it is not in man who walks to direct his steps." Who are we to tell God who, what, when, where, and how? When we gave our lives to Christ, we did just that. God has a plan for all of us. It is through our surrendering and obedience that His will is accomplished.

Surrender and obedience go hand in hand. They are like twins. You can't be obedient if you haven't surrendered your life to Christ. As a consequence, you haven't fully surrendered your life to Christ if you are living in disobedience. I can remember dating a certain fellow. I wasn't sure about him, and I didn't like the way the relationship made me feel at times. I knew that the relationship wasn't from God because it wasn't godly. We would have godly conversations. However, not all the conversations were godly. So I prayed to the Lord about everything, quite a few times. One day after work, I came home, plopped down on my living room sofa, and prayed. I openly expressed to God how I felt about everything. I sat quiet for a moment. As soon as I got quiet, the Holy Spirit said, "Remove yourself from that situation." He didn't say, "I will remove you." He told me to remove myself. Oftentimes God will tell us to do something and we have to surrender in obedience. Of course, it was hard to let go of that "friendship" because I didn't want to be alone. I had finally found some companionship. However, I knew in my heart that if things continued, I would eventually have sex with this person. Therefore, I cut it off.

The Bible says, if you are willing and obedient, you shall eat the good of the land; but if you refuse and rebel, you will be devoured by the sword (Isaiah 1:19-20). We have to be willing to trust God enough to surrender and obey. It is for our protection. I later ran into this person, only to find out that he had sex with his ex-girlfriend and was really dealing with some serious strongholds. I thank God for His covering. My disobedience would have cost me unnecessary heartache.

Don't get me wrong. There have been times where I didn't listen to the voice of God. I did what I wanted to do and paid for it. For example, the Lord had told me to stop dealing with one of my ex-boyfriends. Of course, I didn't want to because, again, I would be alone.

Nevertheless, I continued talking to him and seeing him. I can remember getting ready to go see him one night. I knew that I was dead wrong, because I remember what the Lord had told me prior to this. I'll never forget what I said to God on my way out the door. I said, "I know I shouldn't be going, but I'm going anyway. I'm not staying in this house alone again tonight. Now, cover me Lord as I leave." The nerve of me! Anyway, I went. Maybe an hour after I got there we got into a huge fight about nothing (as always). He cursed me out in the street as if I was a random prostitute. I was so embarrassed, and so angry. He actually put me out of his house. I can remember driving home (which was an hour away). All I could think was, *Why is my life going this way? Why did I come out here to see him?* As I drove home in silence, feeling stupid, the Lord spoke. He said, "See, this is why I didn't want you to come. I didn't want you to get hurt. I don't want anyone yelling at you. I'm not trying to keep anything from you. I'm trying to help you." When God tells you to leave a person alone, be obedient. It is not to make you miserable, but to keep you from unnecessary misery later on. You are God's chosen. Just as you hate being treated wrongly, God hates it even more. I can still remember His tone. It wasn't condescending at all. It was as if God

pitied me. I appreciated the fact that He didn't
scorn me, but counseled me.

I tell that story because after being
disobedient for a long while, I learned to trust
God with my relationships. God allowed me to
suffer different things because of my
disobedience. As a result, I learned to surrender
my will for His. I learned that I couldn't trust
myself to make the right decisions in romantic
relationships. We must seek God for our
relationships. He knows the heart of every man.
So why not heed His voice and surrender?

When we start manipulating things and
people so that we don't have to be alone, we're
not surrendered. If you are still dealing with a
person that God told you was no good for you,
you are not surrendered. If you are still sleeping
around when you know it is wrong, you are not
surrendered. God wants us in our proper place so
He can bless us at the appointed time. How can
He bless you if you are not where you need to be
physically, mentally, and spiritually?

Trusting God is not simply going to
church and busying one's self in ministry. It is
about a relationship—a relationship that is built
on trust. As you surrender to what the Lord is

telling you to do, you will see Him ordering your steps. He will guide your relationships if you let Him. God is practical. He will guide you in the simplest things, even who to date. But you must be receptive and obedient to what He is saying.

Real surrender is being honest with God. It is saying, "God, my life is not my own. I belong to you. However, I don't want to be single. You gave me a desire to be joined to another person. Although I don't want to be alone right now, I accept your will. I know that there is a reason why it hasn't happened yet. Help me to make wise choices in the meantime and seek Your will for this season of my life." I know this is not easy, especially when it seems like every day someone else is getting married while you're getting older. We have to remember God's timing is not our timing. (See Chapter 3). His time is the best time. He knows what is around the corner. Therefore, we must learn to surrender even our timetable to the Lord. I knew I would be married by the time I was 30. At the age of 24, everything was going according to plan—my plan that is. After 24 everything changed. Even then I still believed that God would send my "Mr. Right" before I was 31 years old. Wrong! I still had some growing up to do. I still had to learn who God was, is, and will always be in my life.

If we are not surrendered to Christ, we are full of pride. Pride is the opposite of humility. It takes humility to surrender to God's will. If you won't surrender, you are saying to God, "You don't know what you're doing. I should be married by now. I should have children by this time." You are telling God that you can run your own life and you don't need Him. What kind of follower of Christ is that? Understand that God is God and we are but dust. We don't know everything. Trust God with your life. For the eyes of the LORD run to and fro throughout the whole earth, to show Himself strong on behalf of *those* whose heart *is* loyal to Him (2 Chronicles 16:9). He will show Himself strong on your behalf if you will trust Him and surrender.

It's not by accident that you are single. God is in control. Furthermore, if you have been disobedient and not surrendered to Christ, I urge you to get back in line. It's never too late for God to turn things around for you. We, as humans, don't know what God is doing unless He reveals it. Therefore, total trust and surrender is essential. We must emulate our Savior, our

Brother, our Example, Jesus Christ, when He said to the Father, "If it is Your will, take this cup away from Me; nevertheless not My will, but Yours, be done." (Luke 22:42). Choose to do the will of God. He will reward your sacrifice and your obedience. Just as God tested Abraham to offer his beloved son, He will test us. Abraham was willing to sacrifice his only son, whom he waited years to receive. But God was faithful to bless Abraham as he surrendered to God in obedience (Genesis 22). He will be faithful to us as we surrender and offer our sacred desires up to Him.

Remember, you belong to Christ. Your life is not your own. Surrender.

2

GET IN HIS
PRESENCE

2

GET IN HIS PRESENCE

Seek the LORD while He may be found; Call upon Him while He is near.

Isaiah 55:6

I know what it feels like to want to be held by another person. I understand that this journey is not a walk in the park. However, God's grace is sufficient (2 Corinthians 12:9). As singles, we have more opportunities to get closer to God than married people do. As we lie in bed alone we can talk to God. We can freely pace the floor at 3 AM worshipping the Lord. Those without children can come home after work to spend time in His Word, uninterrupted. Personally, I've learned to take advantage of being able to pray in the middle of the night. I'm able to speak with God one on one anytime I am ready. God desires us in His presence. Instead of sulking about the spouse we don't have, we should look to our Heavenly Father. We are married to God for all eternity. The Bible says,

"Your Maker is your Husband." (Isaiah 54:5). We should treat Him as such. We should spend time in His presence to get know Him. When we are in the presence of God, we are able to hear Him to receive instruction and correction. Many of us need healing and deliverance. The healing and deliverance that you need, will only come from the presence of God, not man.

We need to know that in His presence, He will hear and answer us. God is able to open our ears and understanding. "The Lord GOD has given me the tongue of the learned, that I should know how to speak a word in season to *him who is* weary. He awakens me morning by morning; He awakens my ear to hear as the learned. The Lord GOD has opened My ear; and I was not rebellious, nor did I turn away." (Isaiah 50:4-5). He is able to lead us in this season of our lives. If left to our own fleshly desires and understanding, we will fail God. We will miss what God is doing in this season. As I surrendered to God, I sought Him more. I sought His Face more. I began to seek from God what He desires for me. I know that God is a God of purpose, so I knew that I had purpose for this season of my life. I went before the Lord often to ask what I was to birth in this season, as you should. God has a purpose for this season of your life. Get in His presence to find out what it is.

If we desire God, surely we can have Him. God says, "Then you will seek Me, inquire for, *and* require Me [as a vital necessity] and find Me when you search for Me with all your heart." (Jeremiah 29:13). The problem with some of us is that we are more concerned about getting another date than we are with seeking God with our whole hearts. God must be your vital necessity. The scriptures advise us to, "draw near to God and He will draw near to us." (James 4:8). We must draw near to the One who is able to bless us with instruction and correction. So many times we look to people as our source for advice or attention when God is waiting for us to turn to Him. How can you hear God if you are not listening to Him? How can you know what God is telling you to do if you never make time for Him? In 2 Chronicles 7:14 God says, "If My people who are called by My name will humble themselves, and pray and seek My face, and turn from their wicked ways, then I will hear from Heaven, and will forgive their sin and heal their land." We must learn to humble ourselves enough to seek God for His will and His way, especially as singles. We are tempted everyday by passions of the flesh, and we need to be in God's presence more than ever.

Apart from God, we are not wise. Were you present to hear the secret counsel of God? And do you limit [the possession of] wisdom to yourself (Job 15:8)? Sometimes when we get tired of waiting on God, we leave His presence. We go ahead of God, make a costly mistake, and then blame God. God's character is consistent. He never changes (Malachi 3:6). We walk away and do things on our own because we are not in the presence of God like we ought to be. For some of us it's harder to be single. Some people struggle more than others. Nevertheless, I believe if we get in the habit of seeking God, He will keep us. He will bless us with His presence. The Lord is near to all who call upon Him, to all who call upon Him in truth (Psalm 145:18). We need to call upon God in truth, which is on the foundation of His Word. Some singles are single parents and live on a low or fixed income. If that's you, then you must call upon God based on His Word. God said you are the head and not the tail (Deuteronomy 28:13). You shall lend and not borrow (Deuteronomy 15:6). Get closer to God and speak His Word over your life. Nothing is more important. I know sometimes you get lonely and nothing will do except another person. The truth is, man can't bless us unless God gives him the resources to do so. Man doesn't have the capacity to open doors that no one can shut. Man can't bless you with healing and deliverance. God may use people as a resource, but the truth is, **God is your SOURCE**. He is the source of all good things (James 1:17).

I have gotten so frustrated with being single sometimes I didn't even want to talk to God. It was in those moments I knew that I needed God the most. I knew that if I would just go into worship or sit in the house of God on a Tuesday night, His presence would make a difference. The truth is, it does make a difference. There is nothing like the still and peaceful presence of God.

It's good to pray and ask God for a godly spouse. But some are asking for a godly spouse and are not living a godly lifestyle ourselves. Some want to go to the bar and hang in the streets flirting, all the while asking God for a godly marriage. How can this be? As I spent more time in God's presence, the Holy Spirit told me to "be who I am praying for." **Be who you are praying for.** If you want a godly spouse that seeks God, you need to be a godly person who seeks God. If you want a mate who spends time in God's presence, you need to spend time in God's presence. If you want a mate that fasts and prays, what do you think you need to do? If God sends you the person that you are praying for and you are not where you need to be (spiritually, emotionally, and mentally) they may not want you. I had to be real with myself and ask, "Would I marry me?" Many times I said no! I began to understand that God's presence is where I needed to dwell. I knew that I needed to become the woman God desired me to be, so that He can send the man He desired me to have. Therefore, I decided to change my mind and get closer to God.

Make a permanent decision to stay in God's presence. I know being single is not your first option. However, let us look at this hypothetical scenario. You get married and you live your life with this person for X amount of years. God forbid something terrible happens like divorce or they suddenly die. You will be single again, unless you die first. *You will still need God.* I know this is a bit drastic, but it is realistic. God will always be there, spouse or no spouse. God will keep us safe in His presence. He will advise us about who to have in our lives. He will restore and heal us. Get in His presence!

Here are some scriptures on the presence of God. Please read these prayerfully and allow God to draw you into His presence.

Psalm 31:20 - In the secret place of Your presence You hide them from the plots of men; You keep them secretly in Your pavilion from the strife of tongues.

Psalm 25:4-5 - Show me your ways, LORD, teach me your paths. Guide me in your truth and teach me, for you are God my Savior, and my hope is in you all day long.

Psalm 16:11 - You will show me the path of life; in Your presence is fullness of joy, at Your right hand there are pleasures forevermore.

Psalm 73:28 - But it is good for me to draw near to God; I have put my trust in the Lord God *and* made Him my refuge, that I may tell of all Your works.

1 Chronicles 16:27 - Honor and majesty are [found] in His presence; strength and joy are [found] in His sanctuary.

Jeremiah 29:13 - Then you will seek Me, inquire for, *and* require Me [as a vital necessity] and find Me when you search for Me with all your heart.

Revelation 3:20 - Here I am! I stand at the door and knock. If anyone hears my voice and opens the door, I will come in and eat with that person, and they with me.

Exodus 33:14 - And the Lord said, My Presence shall go with you, and I will give you rest.

3

GOD'S TIMING

3

GOD'S TIMING

*For the vision is yet for an appointed time and it
hastens to the end [fulfillment]; it will not
deceive or disappoint. Though it tarry, wait
[earnestly] for it, because it will surely come; it
will not be behindhand on its appointed day.*

Habakkuk 2:3

I am an ambitious person. I'm very
independent. I like to do things my own way in
my own time. Surrendering my will to God was
and is hard at times. Sometimes I get frustrated
because I figure I can do things on my own and
have it done in half the time. However, the Bible
tells me, "He has made everything beautiful in its
time." (Eccl. 3:11). At the right time, God will
bless you and it will be beautiful.

If God has told you that you will be
married, then so shall it be. You can count on it.
For all the promises of God in Him *are* Yes, and
in Him Amen, to the glory of God through us (2

Corin. 1:20). When God releases that Word in the atmosphere, it's an activation of what has already been predestined to happen. He uses His prophets to set the clock because it's only a matter of *time* before the manifestation takes place. At that point, it's a countdown until the appointed time. God says in Isaiah 55:11, "So shall My word be that goes forth from My mouth; It shall not return to Me void, But it shall accomplish what I please, And it shall prosper *in the thing* for which I sent it."

Many times in my own life, I've wondered why I was not married yet. Why didn't God choose me to go through something else? Why this? Why can't my life be "perfect" like those I see on television? I realize now that God has a purpose for me. I will marry at the appointed time set by God to accomplish His purpose on Earth. We have to understand that we are a part of God's plan of salvation. He wants to bless us, but it must be on His time. Of course, we can go outside the will of God. We can marry and have children by who we want without His direction. Nevertheless, this is NOT the will of God.

Case in point, Abraham and Sarah in the Old Testament had no children. God appeared to Abraham in a vision. Abraham brought his case about being childless before the Lord. God then promised him a seed from his own body (Genesis 15). At this time Abraham was an old man. However, the Bible says in Genesis 15:6, "And he [Abram] believed in (trusted in, relied on, remained steadfast to) the Lord, and He counted it to him as righteousness (right standing with God)." So he believed God would do as He promised. After many years, Sarah and Abraham became impatient with God's timing and moved on their own. Sadly, this is what many of God's people do today. Sarah asked her husband to sleep with her maid, Hagar, so they may have children—so he did. Hagar became pregnant and bore Ishmael, which caused strife between Sarah and Hagar. When we do things in our flesh, we bring on ourselves unnecessary aggravation. Ishmael was not the son that God promised Abraham. However, God allowed Hagar to become pregnant. Sometimes God will allow things to happen, which is called God's permissive will. It's not what God wants, but He allows it because He gives us the freedom to choose. And besides that, God is still able to allow it to work out for your good. In this instance, Abraham and Sarah chose what they thought was best. They were not surrendered to God's timing. Surrender is essential in this journey with God. (See Chapter 1).

Two chapters later, the Lord appears to
Abraham again and confirms His Word about his
wife bearing him a son (Genesis 17). The
promise was yet to be fulfilled, but God is true to
His Word. More time passes, but in Chapter 18,
the Lord appeared to Abraham in the form of
men and said, "'I will certainly return unto thee
according to the time of life; and, lo, Sarah thy
wife shall have a son." And Sarah heard it in the
tent door, which was behind him." (Genesis
18:10). Some words in this scripture jumped out
at me as I read them. The angel of the Lord said,
"ACCORDING TO THE TIME OF LIFE."

Know this: God is beyond time. He
created it, but He does not need to operate
according to it as we do. We are restricted by
time; God is not. He respects it, but He is not
bound to it. Don't forget, He is able to redeem
time. (Joel 2:25).

"But, beloved, be not ignorant of this one
thing, that one day is with the Lord as a thousand
years, and a thousand years as one day." (2 Peter
3:8). We are on Earth. In the earth God has set
time to keep us in accordance with His purpose.
"To everything, there is a season, and a time to
every purpose under the Heaven." (Ecclesiastes
3:1). Timing and purpose are like cousins. If we
do something out of season, it will not be

fruitful. As a result, the purpose of God is not fulfilled according to His will. You can't plant seeds in the winter and expect a fruitful harvest. Know the time and season you are in so that you might be fruitful. We must seek God about His timing for our lives.

I know some people have waited all their life for God to bless them with a spouse. Some have waited 10, 15, 20 years for a spouse. Some are saying, "God, where is your promise?" What do we do when the promise seems afar off? What do we do when it seems there is no light at the end of the tunnel? Pray and have faith in God's timing. God is faithful. We must also remain faithful in waiting. After waiting such a long time to receive the promise of a son, Sarah conceived. The Bible says in Hebrews 11:11, "through faith also Sara herself received strength to conceive seed, and was delivered of a child when she was past age, because she judged Him faithful who had promised." The one thing she desired most, which seemed impossible after such a long wait, God performed. Our God is faithful. If we are faithless (do not believe and are untrue to Him), He remains true (faithful to His Word and His righteous character), for He cannot deny Himself (2 Timothy 2:13). If this scripture doesn't encourage you, I don't know

what will. Even when we are faithless and
unfaithful to Him, He remains faithful. Don't
give up. Trust God's timing.

One scripture that has blessed me
throughout this journey (which you will see
several times in this book) is **Psalm 84:11**. **"For
the LORD God is a sun and shield; the LORD
will give grace and glory; no good thing will
He withhold from them that walk uprightly."**
This is a promise that I recite to myself often. It
is conditional because it is for those that walk
uprightly, but it is a promise from God. Another
scripture that keeps me is **Psalm 34:10**. **"The
young lions lack food and suffer hunger, but
they who seek (inquire of and require) the
Lord [by right of their need and on the
authority of His Word], none of them shall
lack any beneficial *thing*."** Continue to wait on
God.

As I struggled with God's time in my
own wait, God led me to examine the story of
Joseph. God began to show me things that
encouraged me about His timing. God's timing
and purpose had a lot to do with Joseph's
confinement. He was a slave in Potiphar's house
(although God blessed him) and he was confined
in prison. God placed purpose in Joseph at the
age of 17. However, that purpose didn't manifest

until He reigned in Egypt at the age of 30. Can you imagine how frustrated this man was? Although God's favor was with Joseph wherever he went, he was not a free man. He'd been separated from his family and all that he knew at a young age. I can only imagine how much he missed his father terribly. Nevertheless, it was all a part of God's plan. We must remember this truth in our waiting season.

The amount of time that Joseph was confined was very significant to what God wanted to do in Egypt. He couldn't be released from prison too soon or too late. It had to be at the time (the appointed time) that God would reveal to the king in his dreams His plans for Egypt. So even when the chief butler was released from prison and forgot about Joseph, it was a part of Gods' plan (Genesis 40). It was not time for Joseph's purpose. He had to be released during the seven years of plenty and seven years of famine in Egypt. Every dream, every desire that God showed Joseph was valid. However, it was not the time for validation. He had to wait and trust God. In my mind, I can see Joseph pacing the floors of his cell at night, worshipping the Lord. He was staying hopeful and maintaining his integrity during his waiting. All the while, guilty people were being released ahead of schedule; people were going home to see their families, but not Joseph. He had to endure this hurtful experience. As I looked at this, I realized that Joseph's time of confinement had nothing to do with him. It had everything to do with God's purpose.

Those of us who are waiting on the promise of God for a spouse, must continue to wait. Our waiting has everything to do with God's purpose in our lives and in the lives of others. Honestly, this is a hard one for me. I don't even like the word wait. I don't like to wait for anything. But I know God's timing is perfect. He knows what He is doing. He sees what we cannot see. He knows what's ahead. He knows the plans He has for us. He has plans to prosper and not to harm us, plans to give us hope and a future (Jeremiah 29:11).

Here are some scriptures to meditate on as you wait on God:

Isaiah 40:28-31 - Have you not known? Have you not heard? The everlasting God, the Lord, the Creator of the ends of the earth, does not faint or grow weary; there is no searching of His understanding. He gives power to the faint *and* weary, and to him who has no might He increases strength [causing it to multiply and making it to abound]. Even youths shall faint and be weary, and [selected] young men shall feebly stumble *and* fall exhausted; But those who wait for the Lord [who expect, look for, and hope in Him] shall change *and* renew their strength *and* power; they shall lift their wings *and* mount up [close to God] as eagles [mount up to the sun]; they shall run and not be weary, they shall walk and not faint *or* become tired.

Lamentations 3:24-25 - The Lord is my portion *or* share, says my living being (my inner self); Therefore, will I hope in Him *and* wait expectantly for Him. The Lord is good to those who wait hopefully *and* expectantly for Him, to those who seek Him [inquire of and for Him and require Him by right of necessity and on the authority of God's word].

Psalm 27:13 - [What, what would have become of me] had I not believed that I would see the Lord's goodness in the land of the living!

Isaiah 64:4 - For from of old no one has heard nor perceived by the ear, nor has the eye seen a God besides You, Who works *and* shows Himself active on behalf of him who [earnestly] waits for Him.

God is an active God. He acts on behalf of those who wait for Him. The thing is, we must learn to wait. If we want God's best, we have to wait for it. Of course, everyone's wait is not the same length of time. This is because everyone's journey and purpose in God is different. That's why we shouldn't waste our time envying other people's lives. (See Chapter 8).

As we seek God about our lives, we should seek Him about His timing. I know you get weary at times. And nobody seems to understand your weariness. Though the Bible says, "let us not lose heart *and* grow weary *and* faint in acting nobly *and* doing right, **for in due time *and* at the appointed season we shall reap**, if we do not loosen *and* relax our courage *and* faint." (Galatians 6:9). We will reap if we faint not. Don't give up. Even if you have to cry all night, don't give up on God. Wait for Him. Those who sow in tears shall reap in joy (Psalm 126:5). So cry if you must, but cry out to God.

Know that there is nothing too hard for God. What is impossible with men is possible with God (Luke 18:27). What seems impossible because of the timing is possible for God. Don't die in your wilderness; keep moving in faith trusting God's timing. He is always on time. HE HAS MADE EVERYTHING BEAUTIFIL IN ITS TIME (Ecclesiastes 3:11). When your time comes, it will be beautiful. Be encouraged as you wait on the Lord's timing.

Wait *and* hope for *and* expect the Lord; be brave *and* of good courage and let your heart be stout *and* enduring. Yes, wait for *and* hope for *and* expect the Lord (Psalm 27:14).

4

LONELY DAYS

4

LONELY DAYS

Come to Me, all you who labor and are heavy laden, and I will give you rest. Take My yoke upon you and learn from Me, for I am gentle and lowly in heart, and you will find rest for your souls.

Matthew 11:28-29

I have had more lonely days than I'd care to admit. Whether I am in a sanctuary full of people or at home alone, I have felt the sting of loneliness. Some Sundays after church, I couldn't bear the thought of going home to an empty house. I dreaded some days after work because I knew I would be home alone. The truth is, we must remember that God is always with us. His Spirit lives in us so we are never alone. By this we know that we abide in Him, and He in us, because He has given us of His Spirit (1 John 4:13).

There are many Friday and Saturday nights that I spend alone. Of course I spend time with family and friends, but some days it doesn't suffice. I've cried many days and nights praying to God for a change. Holidays like Thanksgiving and Christmas can be torture. There have been times when I've enjoyed myself, but deep down I was disappointed because I longed for something that seemed beyond my reach. Many times I swore I would date the next person who asked me out. I said, "This is crazy. I shouldn't have to be alone. I'm just gonna do my thing. No harm in that." Then the Holy Spirit would always remind me that I had a choice: obey God and wait, or do my own thing and miss God. Therefore, I continue to wait on God. I made the decision to become celibate. I had made this decision before but failed numerous times. This has been a challenge, but God has kept me thus far. Sometimes I think to myself, *How in the world am I doing this?* The truth is, it is God's Spirit enabling me to do it. After God sent the word to me about my husband through one of his prophets, I got serious. I believed God. Even in my lonely times when it seemed no one cared or understood, I still believed God. I believed God would deliver and bless me. Deep down I knew He cared. Just as He cares for me, He cares for you.

The lonely days are days when we need to get into the presence of God. He's always present. They are not the times to have pity parties or get on the phone with your friend and complain, but times to seek God's presence. In His presence is fullness of joy (Psalm 16:11). These are the times to get to know God. These are the times to get to know the heart of God. It is in His presence that He will advise, comfort, and direct you, if you will just get there. In Matthew 11:28, Jesus says come to Him. He will give us rest for our souls. You need rest. You need rest from wrestling with your single state, from worrying, and from comparing yourself to others. (See Chapter 9). You need to rest in God's presence when you feel lonely. He will give you new ideas, a new perspective, new strength, and new vigor to live this life.

The Bible says, "the Lord spoke to Moses face to face, as a man speaks to his friend." (Exodus 33:11). I love that! If God is the same yesterday, today, and forevermore (Hebrews 13:8), why would He not give us the same privilege? It is up to us to shake off the loneliness and get into the presence of God. How can we get close to another human being without getting close to our Heavenly Father first?

Bible giants like David, endured loneliness. He says, "reproach has broken my heart, and I am full of heaviness; I looked *for someone* to take pity, but *there was* none; and for comforters, but I found none." (Psalm 69:20). Regardless, David carried on and cried out to God for help and comfort. God is your Comforter, your Strength, and your Helper if you allow Him to be. "Behold He who keeps Israel shall neither slumber nor sleep." (Psalm 121:4). The Lord is always near. Just because you can't see or feel Him doesn't mean He isn't with you. Trust, believe, and have faith in Him who has called you to such a time.

Getting into the presence of God is a great remedy for combating loneliness. In addition to that, concerning yourself with the needs of others is helpful. We can choose to sit and pout about how long God is taking and why we aren't married yet. Or we can look in the Body of Christ for those that are hurting and less fortunate. We can choose to help someone else.

When Jesus was 12 years old His family took their annual trip to Jerusalem at the Feast of Passover. After their trip they began their journey home only to find that Jesus was not with them. When they eventually found Him, He was at the Temple in Jerusalem sitting in the midst of scholars. His mother said to Him, "Son, why have You done this to us? Look, Your father and I have sought You anxiously." Then Jesus said to His mother, "Why did you seek Me? Did you not know that I must be about My Father's business?" (Luke 2:41-49). We need not concern ourselves with the things of this life but be about our Father's business. I'm convinced that if we take care of God's business He will take care of ours. Pray and ask God to help you right now. You are meant to be alone for this season of your life, but not lonely.

After all the pity parties and frustration, I realized I couldn't pray away God's timing. Once I began to seek Him about my purpose in this season, I took my eyes off myself. I still have my days when I get lonely, but I realize that I have purpose in this season. (See Chapter 23). I used my time to get my bachelors and masters degrees. I figured, "Why not redeem the time and develop myself?" In addition, the Lord told me to revive the singles ministry at my church. Therefore, I became the leader for that ministry. He also placed it in my heart to write this book to help other singles in the Body of Christ. Find someone to help. Find someone who needs your prayers. Seek ways to contribute to your church. Develop yourself as a successful individual so when God does send your mate, he or she is in awe of you.

Let's face it; when we feel lonely, sometimes we become desperate. The enemy likes to come in when we are feeling lonely. It makes it easier for him to get into your mind and tell lies. I can remember feeling lonely and down in the dumps listening to the lies of the enemy. I could hear him say, "It's never going to happen. Why are you still waiting? Why are you still serving God? If He was going to bless you it would have happened by now." The enemy would also show me couples that aren't saved but are happily married and say, "But you're still waiting on God, though? Okay, keep waiting." It's imperative that we guard our minds when we are alone. (See Chapter 11). In our loneliness, we can begin to believe the lies of the enemy, become desperate, and engage in relationships that God never intended for us to engage in. When we feel lonely, we do desperate things. You become desperate and you find yourself scrolling down the address book in your cell phone to call an ex. In addition, you start texting people God told you to leave alone. You begin taking dates from "randoms" that you know aren't saved. You must guard your feelings. People that we were delivered from seem to come back around at our most desperate times. Don't be deceived by the enemy's tactics. Pray, seek God in His word, and ask God to help you in those desperate moments. It can save you from regret and heartache later on.

When we become familiar with "being with someone" we can develop a dependence on that person. Companionship is great, but we should not depend on people to make us feel good or fill any voids in our lives. Only Jesus can fill every void. If we depend on people to fulfill needs that only God can, we will be disappointed every time. In our time alone we need to learn to depend on the presence of God to make us whole. In my loneliest moments God was there. I knew that if I wanted to remain in the will of God and be obedient then I had to endure. I had to surrender. I used my time alone to study the Word of God, pray, and enter into worship. I used that time to get closer to God. (See Chapter 2).

No doubt about it, you will feel lonely at times. It is up to you how you react to it. If you need to cry, then cry. If you need to shout, then shout. However, don't stop there. Seek God and ask for His help. Ask God to fill your voids. If you have to keep asking, then keep asking. God doesn't get tired of us coming to Him. Be not consumed by this fiery trial. God says, "Fear not, for I *am* with you; Be not dismayed, for I *am* your God. I will strengthen you, Yes, I will help you, I will uphold you with My righteous right hand." (Isaiah 41:10).

Choose how you will react to your alone time. Know that God has a blessed purpose for everything He does. *We know that all things work together for the good of those who love God—those whom He has called according to his plan.* (Romans 8:28, GW). So be encouraged and take full advantage of your time alone with your Everlasting Father. He's waiting.

5

THE ISOLATION CHAMBER

5

THE ISOLATION CHAMBER

Not forsaking or neglecting to assemble together
[as believers], as is the habit of some people, but
admonishing [warning, urging, and
encouraging] one another, and all the more
faithfully as you see the day approaching.

Hebrews 10:25

There is a difference between God
isolating us from some people and us isolating
ourselves from others. To isolate yourself is to
separate yourself from others. An isolation
chamber is like solitary confinement. You are
left alone with your own thoughts, opinions,
fears, and lack of faith. There is no contact with
your brothers and sisters in Christ. You are left
alone to deal with your problems. Many times I
felt depressed and I just wanted to be left alone. I
would isolate myself from everyone. I didn't
care how anyone else felt about it. However, the
Bible advises us to forsake not the assembly of
the saints (Hebrews 10:25). Why do you think

that is? God knows when we are isolated from the remainder of the body, we cannot function properly. He knows that the enemy can easily attack us. Put on God's whole armor [the armor of a heavy-armed soldier which God supplies], that you may be able successfully to stand up against [all] the strategies *and* the deceits of the devil (Ephesians 6:11). Isolation is one of the strategies the enemy uses to hinder our growth, deliverance, and prosperity.

If you are isolating yourself, know that you are not operating in wisdom. He who willfully separates *and* estranges himself [from God and man] seeks his own desire *and* pretext to break out against all wise *and* sound judgment (Proverbs 18:1). Before I sought God about my assignment in this season, I didn't want to talk to anyone; I wanted to do my own thing. I definitely didn't want to hear any sermons. I was fed up and felt life was just unfair. When you are isolated, it is easy to have pity parties and give up. We need to be around others that encourage us. We need to be around other like-minded individuals so we can know we are not alone in this thing.

The truth is, we have brothers and sister all over the world who share the same burdens. If we isolate ourselves from other believers we will never know it. I can remember always staying home from church. I would slip into a deep depression for days. I would lie in bed all day in a daze. I would take sleeping pills and wash them down with alcohol to ease the pain of the many emotional scars. Many of those scars were left by past mistakes and hurts that I had not dealt with. The more I stayed isolated, the more I gave in to negative thoughts and the more I became depressed. The longer I was depressed, the longer I stayed away from the house of God. The enemy knows what he is doing. If he can get you isolated and depressed, he can get you to stay away from the house of God. There is deliverance in the house of God. There is deliverance in the prayers of the saints. Of course you can pray over the phone, but there is something about the prayer of agreement in person. There is nothing like the fire of God in the midst of praying saints! God says, "For where two or three are gathered together in my name, there am I in the midst of them." (Matthew 18:20).

Don't make the mistake of thinking you can make it on your own. You need to be around people that are struggling but holding on to the promises of God. I can remember going to church listening to some of the testimonies and struggles of others. It blew my mind as these people were still faithful to God in ministry and in their faith. It made me want to hold on just a little bit longer. It gave me the strength to bear my burdens. The blessings of God are not always material. They are also spiritual. We are blessed by other believers as they witness about what God has done in their lives. We become stronger as we unite with other believers in the faith.

I often wanted to sit home, read the Bible, and watch a sermon or two on television to suffice for the presence of God in His house. I didn't feel like being fake or phony. I just wanted to be left alone to be depressed. I figured I could read the Bible and get what I needed that way. However, God places a special anointing on His preachers and teachers that they may deliver the Word with revelation, conviction, and deliverance. In Acts Chapter 8 it explains the story of how Philip preached to an Ethiopian. The Spirit of the Lord lured the disciple Philip to this man. As the Ethiopian read the book of the prophet Isaiah, the Bible says Philip ran to him and heard him reading it, and asked, "Do you understand what you are reading?" And he said, "How can I, unless someone guides me?" And he invited Philip to come up and sit with him (Acts 8:30-31). We need teaching. We need to be where the anointing of God is. As singles we need fellowship. We need the church and the church needs us.

While we are single, we have more time on our hands (unless you have children). Married people have but so much time to give to the church. As singles we should be the busiest in the church. We should be the main ones evangelizing, ministering, feeding the homeless, etc. Singles should be on the front line for Christ instead of crying about how unfair life is. We really need to be about our Father's business. We are single for such a time as this. This is the season to make an impact on those around you. This is the time to allow God to use you in a significant way. Delight yourself also in the Lord, and He will give you the desires *and* secret petitions of your heart. Commit your way to the Lord [roll and repose each care of your load on Him]; trust (lean on, rely on, and be confident) also in Him and He will bring it to pass (Psalm 37:4-5). We must trust God and get busy for the Kingdom of God.

I'm always reminded of Ruth's character, even as a widow, in the book of Ruth. Her husband had died and she was in a foreign land living with her deceased husband's mother. Of

63

course she wanted children and a husband of her own, but her focus was different. She wanted to help her mother-in law. As soon as she arrived in Bethlehem, she got busy working. And Ruth the Moabitess said to Naomi, Let me go to the field and glean among the ears of grain after him in whose sight I shall find favor. Naomi said to her, Go, my daughter (Ruth 2:2). She didn't hesitate. She wasn't crying over what wasn't. She was strong, full of courage, and focused. Observe how Boaz noticed Ruth. She didn't have to switch passed him or dress provocatively to grab his attention. **Then Boaz said to his servant who was set over the reapers, Whose maiden is this? (Ruth 2:5).** If we focus on the things of God, God will send to us what is rightfully ours. **And Boaz said to her, I have been made fully aware of all you have done for your mother-in-law since the death of your husband, and how you have left your father and mother and the land of your birth and have come to a people unknown to you before (Ruth 2:11).** I love this! She didn't have to impress him with her background, her clothes, her body, or her status. He was drawn to her by her good works and noble character.

Get out of your isolation chamber and get busy for God! There is no time to waste. I know things may seem rough right now, but God is our Redeemer. He will redeem your life. Have faith, be bold, and serve God with all your heart. Ask God by His Holy Spirit to lead you where He wants you to go in ministry and in your relationships. Don't continue to isolate yourself. God made us for each other. You need the Body of Christ and the Body of Christ needs you.

6

THE PIT OF SELF-PITY

6

THE PIT OF SELF-PITY

*Pray without ceasing, in everything give thanks;
for this is the will of God in Christ Jesus for you.*

1 Thessalonians 5:17-18

It is imperative that we check our emotions. We need to rule over our emotions. If we don't, our emotions will rule over us. We don't live by how we feel, but by our faith in the Living God. The Bible says that the just shall live by faith (Hebrews 10:38). It's easy to look at our circumstances and become down in our spirit. It takes faith to believe God despite what it looks like. Self-pity is selfish. You are only concerned with yourself, your circumstances, and your issues. People who deal with self-pity often have the "woest me" attitude. You will never accomplish anything great if you live with this attitude.

Please understand the "pit" of self-pity. Self-pity leads to depression, and depression can lead to suicide. It's demonic; it's not from God. Self-pity will keep you down. You will never achieve anything great for God because you are too concerned with yourself.

I can remember a time where I felt sorry for myself. I thought everyone was blessed except for me. I would go to work, come home, and climb into bed. Sometimes I would stay in my room for days. I didn't want to be bothered with anyone. I didn't care about anything. All I wanted was for my situation to get better. Sundays would come around and I couldn't care less about church. I didn't want to see anyone. I was embarrassed, tired, and all I kept thinking was, *God, why me?* I was so focused and full of myself. Again, self-pity is selfish.

When a person is single and living in self-pity, all they see are other couples. All they see are the children they are supposed to have. They start to believe that it will never happen. At one point I began to think there was something wrong with me. I couldn't understand why no one wanted me. My self-esteem was steadily dwindling. God showed me that my self-esteem has nothing to do with if a man chooses me because *He* has already chosen me. I felt sorry for myself all the time. Make no mistake about it; if nobody would feel sorry for me, I would

SINGLE, SAVED, & SEEKING HIM

feel sorry for myself. I would always ask God, "Why is my life this way? Why is this person's life so perfect? Why am I alone? Why am I the only one going through this? It's not fair...blah, blah, blah." I began struggling with my classes in school, missing events that would enable me to meet people, etc. All the while, I accomplished nothing. I was not productive. The enemy knows if he can get you in a state of self-pity, you will be useless to the Kingdom of God. You will not be a threat to the kingdom of darkness. We must push past how we feel.

Although complaining seems to be the answer, it makes matters worse. Many times we see how angry the Lord became when the children of Israel complained. Even when it hurts, even when we want to slip into self-pity, we need to offer a sacrifice of praise to God. We are to give thanks in every situation. Thank [God] in everything [no matter what the circumstances may be, be thankful and give thanks], for this is the will of God for you [who are] in Christ Jesus [the Revealer and Mediator of that will] (1 Thessalonians 5:18).

As time passed, I allowed God to change me on the inside. He also placed people in my life that would hold me accountable. You need others that will not join in the pity party, but speak life over you and rebuke you in love, if necessary. Pray and ask God to provide those people. I can remember one Memorial Day weekend, this feeling of self-pity and weariness came upon me. I believed that I would be married by now, it was getting close to summer, and all I wanted was to have a nice Memorial Day weekend with my spouse. I was still single and tired of waiting. I was alone again for another summer. There were cookouts going on but I didn't want to go to any. One of my spiritual sisters called me because she had gone through a similar situation. She counseled me and rebuked me in love. After I got off the phone with her, I realized I needed to stop feeling sorry for myself, get out of the house, and enjoy my life. There were many times I wanted to feel sorry for myself but I couldn't. I had to help out with someone else's ministry or celebrate what God had done in the lives of other people. In other words, God was saying to me, "Life is not all about you." So I say to you, life is not all about you. Celebrate with others, help others, and enjoy your life.

In no way am I diminishing the struggle that we as singles face. It is a hard road. However, self-pity will get you nowhere. We have to understand that we are a chosen people, a royal priesthood (1 Peter 2:9). God chose us for every burden, every struggle, and every hardship just as He chose us for every blessing. He knows what we can manage. Sometimes we think we are the only ones going through something but the devil is a LIAR and the father of lies. The Bible tells us in 1 Peter 5:9 to withstand him; be firm in faith [against his onset—rooted, established, strong, immovable, and determined], knowing that the same (identical) sufferings are appointed to your brotherhood (the whole body of Christians) throughout the world. Look around; you're not the only one going through this.

Follow me into 1 Kings 19. The prophet Elijah had slain all the false prophets of Baal. Word got back to Jezebel. Jezebel sent a message to the prophet that by this time tomorrow she would do to him what he did to the false prophets. This mighty man of God, an anointed prophet, ran for his life. He was so afraid that he asked God to take his life. He couldn't bear it any longer. Elijah then came to a cave and lodged in it. The Word of the Lord came to him, and He said to him, "What are you doing here, Elijah?" He replied, "I have been very jealous for the Lord God of hosts; for the Israelites have forsaken Your covenant, thrown down Your altars, and killed Your prophets with the sword. And I, I only, am left; and they seek my life, to take it away." But God said, "Yet I will leave Myself 7,000 in Israel, all the knees that have not bowed to Baal and every mouth that has not kissed him." When we are suffering, why do we think we are the only ones? God had an assignment for the prophet Elijah. It could not be fulfilled unless Elijah pushed past how he felt and listened to God. God revealed to him that there were 7, 000 others who shared the same burden as he did. Elijah had to shake off the self-pity and get moving.

So, you see, you are not the only one that feels the way you feel. The difference is how you react to your circumstances. Do you believe that God is enough? Do you believe that God can bring your deliverance? Do you believe that God is the great I AM? You must get up and move forward. Learn to stand on the promises of God. Many *are* the afflictions of the righteous, but the LORD delivers him out of them all (Psalm 34:19). This season will not last. Speak life and move forward. Time will not stand still for you because you are sad, lonely, and depressed. Believe God, not your feelings. Don't miss out on life because of where you are right now. Don't waste your life feeling sorry for yourself.

Ask God to restore the joy of His salvation and for a willing spirit (Psalm 51:12). Shake that negative spirit off and get your life back!

7

ARE YOU BITTER OR BETTER?

ARE YOU BITTER OR BETTER?

And she said to them, Call me not Naomi
[pleasant]; call me Mara [bitter], for the
Almighty has dealt very bitterly with me. I went
out full, but the Lord has brought me home again
empty. Why call me Naomi, since the Lord has
testified against me, and the Almighty has
afflicted me?

Ruth 1:20-21

Are you bitter or better due to your
current marital status? In this faith walk, there
will be plenty of times when you become weary
and even disappointed. Some things that God
allows you to face while being single can cause
you to become angry, bitter, and even question
God's presence in your life. If you read the book
of Ruth, Naomi began with a husband and two
sons. God had blessed her with a family of her
own. Due to the famine in the land of Bethlehem
in Judah, they left there and moved to Moab.

When Naomi left her hometown, she had everything she thought she wanted. However, when she returned home, the Lord had taken away everything that was dear to her. If you are like me you would ask, "Now why would God do that?" The Bible says the whole town was stirred when Naomi and Ruth returned to Bethlehem. They asked, "Could this be Naomi?"(Ruth 1:19). They didn't even recognize her when she returned home. In my mind, she had a completely different disposition. She, most likely, let herself go in terms of her appearance, and she probably looked bitter. She had allowed her circumstances to make her bitter and change who she was as a person.

I can relate to Naomi's plight. There were times when I would wake up in the morning absolutely grateful. I would be so busy in ministry that being single didn't affect me. There were times when I was completely content with being home on a Friday night watching a movie by myself. I didn't have to cook for anybody, change any diapers, or be held accountable for anyone else. I was at peace in those times. I had the peace of God that surpasses all understanding. Then there were other times when I would allow my peace to escape me. I would wake up, look to my right, and notice that I was still lying in my bed alone. I would go throughout the week thinking negative thoughts. I would begin speaking words into the atmosphere that were not conducive to what I wanted God to perform in my life. Sometimes I would become just plain tired. I would become tired of waiting. I was tired of doing the right things and seeing no results. I allowed myself to become very bitter, very often. There would be days when I didn't want to go to church and put on a happy face because that's not what I was feeling. I wanted to shut everyone out until I got what I wanted or until I felt better. Sometimes I couldn't even pray because I was so angry with God's timing. I felt like He had let me down in this area of my life. Many times all I could do was utter the words "Help me." I didn't think what God was allowing me to endure was fair. I didn't understand what God was doing. I didn't understand that God had a plan for my life, just as He has a plan for yours.

I've learned that perspective is everything. Just as Naomi didn't know what God was doing, we don't know what God is doing. He had a plan for Naomi and Ruth. Ruth was to be in the bloodline of Jesus Christ. Naomi had a family again with Ruth, Boaz, and the birth of her grandson, Obed. **And the women said to**

Naomi, "Blessed be the Lord, Who has not left you this day without a close kinsman, and may his name be famous in Israel. And may he be to you a restorer of life and a nourisher *and* supporter in your old age, for your daughter-in-law who loves you, who is better to you than seven sons, has borne him." Then Naomi took the child and laid him in her bosom and became his nurse (Ruth 4:14-16). We need to learn to look at our circumstances with a spiritual eye rather than a natural eye. God is always at work, whether it appears that way or not. Life is not fair and everything that happens to us is not always good. But God promised to work all things out for the good of those who love Him and are called according to His purpose (Romans 8:28). This includes you. Your circumstance is not meant to kill you, but to make you better. God knows the plans that He has for you, plans to prosper you and not to harm you, plans to give you hope and a future (Jeremiah 29:11).

Another word for bitterness is resentment. I realize that many times when I didn't want to pray it was because I resented God. I was angry with His timing. I was not happy about the way things were working out for me. Although I was blessed in other areas of my life, still, I was not satisfied. I used to feel as though God was not on my side. I knew that God loved me, but I was still bitter about His way of doing things. I tried hard to pretend not to be bitter, but God knew what was in my heart. I can remember one Sunday I went to church as usual. I was smiling, laughing, and greeting the saints. All the while I felt like I wanted to die. But I kept smiling and kept moving on with my day. Finally, I got home, changed my clothes, and started some household chores. I was standing at the kitchen sink washing dishes and suddenly the mask fell off. I started crying, throwing dishes, and eventually hunched over the sink in pain. Even then, I felt God's presence there. It was as if God was waiting for me to do this. I think He was waiting for me to be honest about my feelings. We have to be open with God. There is no use in pretending. You can fool people, but you can't fool God. God can handle your anger. He understands. The key is to talk to Him. Don't make the mistake of holding back what you feel. This will lead to resentment. We can't afford to resent God. Truth is, He is the only One that is truly on our side for all eternity.

Bitterness will cause you to miss God. The harsh circumstances that God allows in our lives are for our gain. Think of Joseph who went through painful circumstances even though he knew in his youth that he was destined for greatness. Nevertheless, he remained humble. He could have turned bitter and walked away from God. He would have missed all that God had prepared for him. Don't become bitter and turn away from God. There is a greater purpose at stake. Even though Joseph was in unfavorable circumstances, he was being prepared for his future in the palace. God was grooming him for his future position. God is preparing you for your future. This time of testing is to make you better, not bitter. *But let endurance and steadfastness and patience have full play and do a thorough work, so that you may be [people] perfectly and fully developed [with no defects], lacking in nothing* (James 1:4). I know you're probably saying, "Well, you don't know how long I've been waiting. You don't know how unfair life has been to me." You're right, I don't. However, the Creator of Heaven and earth knows. He also knows what He is doing. There is a greater purpose for your life than just getting married. Allow God to use this time to make you into a better person. Trust Him.

Take this time to ask God what He desires from you in this stage of your life. Ask Him to give you a willing heart to do His will.

Spend time with Him. Develop a relationship with Him. Even when you don't feel your best, seek His face. Don't allow bitterness to grow in you. Cut it off at the root now. *See to it that no one falls short of the grace of God and that no bitter root grows up to cause trouble and defile many* (Hebrews 12:15). You may not realize it but others are watching you. Don't allow bitterness to stop the purposes of God in your life and in the lives of others.

If you're feeling the sting of bitterness, repent and ask God for forgiveness. Ask Him for His help and guidance in this time. Surround yourself with people of positive influence. Allow yourself to become connected to those who will speak life into your circumstances and believe God with you. The enemy would love nothing more than to fill you with negative feelings towards God, causing you to become bitter and angry. God doesn't want us bitter; He wants us better.

Meditate on these scriptures:

Hebrews 12:4-8 - In your struggle against sin, you have not yet resisted to the point of shedding your blood. And have you completely forgotten this word of encouragement that addresses you as a father addresses his son? It says, "My son, do not make light of the Lord's discipline, and do not lose heart when he rebukes you, because the Lord disciplines the one he loves, and he chastens everyone he accepts as his son." Endure hardship as discipline; God is treating you as his children. For what children are not disciplined by their father? If you are not disciplined—and everyone undergoes discipline—then you are not legitimate, not true sons and daughters at all.

Hebrews 12:11 - For the time being no discipline brings joy, but seems grievous *and* painful; but afterwards it yields a peaceable fruit of righteousness to those who have been trained by it [a harvest of fruit which consists in righteousness—in conformity to God's will in purpose, thought, and action, resulting in right living and right standing with God].

Hebrews 12:12-13 - So then, brace up *and* reinvigorate *and* set right your slackened *and* weakened *and* drooping hands and strengthen your feeble *and* palsied *and* tottering knees, and cut through *and* make firm *and* plain *and* smooth, straight paths for your feet [yes, make them safe and upright and happy paths that go in the right direction], so that the lame *and* halting [limbs] may not be put out of joint, but rather may be cured.

8

BEWARE:
JEALOUSY & ENVY

8

BEWARE: JEALOUSY & ENVY

Let your conversation be without covetousness;
and be content with such things as ye have: for
he hath said, I will never leave thee, nor forsake
thee.

Hebrews 13:5

You cannot and will not enter into the next season of your life with jealousy and envy in your heart. God will not allow it. I know it's hard to watch all of your family and close friends marry off while you're still waiting. It's even harder to pray and ask God for something only to watch Him bless your neighbor with it right in front of your face. If we're not careful, we can become bitter, jealous, and envious of what others have, rather than submit our will to the Lord.

God showed me that there is much jealousy in the Body of Christ. It's as if some think they serve a different God than others.

They believe that what another has attained is not available to them. Despite that erroneous way of thinking, the Bible tells us that there is no partiality with God (Romans 2:11). Moreover, when a person is jealous of another, they feel threatened, as if what they have will be taken away from them by that person.

The Lord led me to Cain and Abel in regards to jealousy in the Body of Christ. Eve bore Cain first, which meant he was the oldest. So, naturally he felt threatened when Abel was born into the family. He was probably used to getting special treatment and being the only boy. Also, by right, the older of the siblings usually has more privileges than the younger. However, when Abel brought to God a better sacrifice than Cain, Cain became very angry. He was jealous of his younger brother because God chose to bless him for his faithfulness. That is the way some are in the body of Christ. You can't halfway obey God and expect to be blessed, then become jealous of your neighbor when God blesses them for their obedience. God is no respecter of persons (Acts 10:34). What He does for one, He will do for another. Despite what it may seem, God is not like man who shows favoritism. Thus, there is no need to feel threatened or jealous of your neighbor. We all serve the same God. Your brother or sister that's newly engaged or married serves the same God as you. What He did for them He is willing to do for you, too.

God said to Cain in Genesis 4:6-7, "Why are you angry? And why do you look sad, depressed, *and* dejected? If you do well, will you not be accepted? And if you do not do well, sin crouches at your door; its desire is for you, but you must master it." Even with an evil heart, God was still on Cain's side. He tried to comfort and counsel him. He tried to tell Cain how to receive the same favor that his brother had received. Sadly, in the next verse Cain kills his younger brother because he allowed his jealousy to shut out the voice of God. If you do what is right in the eyes of God, you will receive the favor and blessings of God. If you are jealous of another, be honest with God about it and heed His voice immediately. Don't allow jealousy to rule in your heart.

The word envious means feeling bitter and unhappy because of another's advantages, possessions, or fortune. It is the desire to have what someone else has—in other words, coveting. You may have never thought of yourself as an envious person but God is the master at showing us what's in our hearts. God will allow us to watch others being blessed for the very things we ask of Him. Many times He wants to show us what is in our hearts. Other times He wants us to learn to genuinely rejoice with others when they are blessed.

Learning to rejoice with others rather than envy what they have was hard for me. At one point in my life (before I was saved) I thought I had everything I wanted. Therefore, there was no need to envy anyone else. However, when God began to humble me, He removed all those things and people from my life. It was as if I was starting from scratch. As I began to walk with the Lord, my desires changed. I would ask God to give me the desires of my heart. I wanted Him to change my desires to whatever He wanted them to be. As I prayed for these desires to come to pass, He began to bless other people with those same desires. One of those desires was to marry a true man of God that genuinely loved me. Then it seemed as if everyone was getting married—everyone except me. While I knew it was a good thing that God was doing in their lives, deep down I wished it were me instead. I thought God was playing some sort of practical joke on me. I can remember being in church and they would announce yet another wedding or engagement. I clapped and smiled, but in my heart I was questioning God. I thought,

"What is this? Why is God passing me over again? What makes this person so special that they get to be married?" Instead of truly rejoicing with God's people, I was letting my desire to be married make me into an envious, coveting, and bitter person. God reminded me that He will have mercy on whom He will have mercy, and He will have compassion on whom He will have compassion (Romans 9:15). It's not our place to question why and when God blesses another person. Furthermore, you don't know what that person went through to get what they have. You don't know the tests that God allowed them to endure in secret before He blessed them openly.

The Bible says in Romans 12:15 that we should "Rejoice with those who rejoice [sharing others' joy], and weep with those who weep [sharing others' grief]." Instead, we are grieved when others are happy and happy when others are grieved. This does not exhibit godly behavior and will not cause God to answer your prayers any faster. In fact, it may prolong your wait until your heart is right before God. I had to bring those negative feelings to God in prayer. I would say, "God, I'm jealous or envious of this person. I want what they have. Please change my heart. I don't want to be like this. Take this from me."

Of course real change doesn't happen overnight, so I kept going before God in prayer about what was in my heart. I would begin to ask God to bless them even more. God would also give me nice things to say and do for them. I believe that God wants to bless me, too. Therefore, I refuse to let envy and jealousy reign in my heart.

The bottom line is this: God loves us. He wants to bless us but our hearts must be right before Him. God desires more for us. He requires a higher standard of living. 1 Corinthians 3:3 says, "For you are still [unspiritual, having the nature] of the flesh [under the control of ordinary impulses]. For as long as [there are] envying and jealousy *and* wrangling and factions among you, are you not unspiritual *and* of the flesh, behaving yourselves after a human standard *and* like mere (unchanged) men?" Heathens allow envy, jealousy, and strife to arise among them. That is not our character as children of God. I pray that you will honestly seek God about any envy or jealousy in your heart, and that you may be delivered and be at peace.

9

COMPARSIONS

9

COMPARISONS

When Peter saw him, he said to Jesus, Lord,
what about this man? Jesus said to him, If I want
him to stay [survive and live] until I come, what
is that to you? [What concern is it of yours?]
You follow Me!

John 21:21-22

The easiest way to become discouraged
and discontented is to compare your life to the
lives of others. When you consume yourself with
the affairs of others, you become distracted from
your own life. Sometimes this is a good thing
and other times it is not. In this case, it is not
because comparing yourself to another is foolish
in the eyes of God. Worrying about what God is
doing in everyone else's lives will cause you to
take your eyes off what God is doing in your life.
In John 21:15-22, the Bible records how Jesus
reinstated Paul even after his denial of Him. This
was a big deal. The Lord had just given him

another chance, a new start, and orders to "take care of His sheep." (John 21:16). However, when Peter noticed another one of the disciples following behind them, he became concerned about what Jesus' plans were for this other person. Jesus kindly told Peter to mind his own business and follow Him (I'm paraphrasing). Many times, we miss God because we are too concerned with what God is doing for others. We don't see the great things that He is doing in our own lives because we are too busy comparing ourselves to other people. I'm sure Peter was ecstatic with his new reinstatement. He probably felt like a new man. Suppose Jesus would have given this other disciple a different assignment that "seemed" more important than Peter's (in Peter's eyes). His contentment, excitement, and peace about what the Lord had just done for him would have escaped him because of comparing.

In my journey as a single Christian, I oftentimes consumed myself with what God was doing in the lives of others. I couldn't understand why some people got married before I did. I didn't like the fact that God would bless unsaved people with happy marriages while I was still waiting on Him for a spouse. I compared myself with people from my past if they were married. By comparing my life to others, I was causing myself to feel less than valuable. I would always ask God why He would bless certain individuals and not me. I didn't understand the ways or the will of God. Certainly it was not God's will that I compare myself to another. Likewise, it is not God's will that you do it. The future that God has planned for your life is unique. He thought about you before the foundations of the earth was formed. He knit you together in your mother's womb (Psalm 139:13). This means that God had plans for you before you even knew He existed. His thoughts towards you are precious and many in number (Psalm 139:17-18). Surely, if God intends for you to marry, God has ordained your spouse, the timing, and the purpose of the marriage. All the days ordained for you were written in His book before one of them came to be (Psalm 139:16). So if this is the case, why burden yourself with comparing your life to another's?

I know it's difficult to continue to wait on the Lord when you find out another one of your friends is engaged. It leads you to question God and His sovereignty. It can become heart wrenching to watch family and friends marry while you still believe God. Nevertheless, you must not compare yourself with others. You must simply congratulate them and continue to believe God for yourself. God may be testing you to see how you will react. You need to get to the point where you have peace because God, in His own time, will bless you. You must stop comparing yourself to those around you before it becomes an even larger problem. Let's say you never get a handle on comparing your life with others'. Where will it end? Once you get married, you will compare your spouse, your house, your children, your children's school, etc. The list goes on. There is no peace in living that way. I often had to talk to myself and say, "I won't compare myself to anyone else. I know God is working in my life, as well. I know His plans for me are good. I will be grateful for the life I have instead of burdening myself with comparisons." Focus on the will of God for **your** life.

I'm reminded of Peter in Matthew 14 as Jesus enabled him walk on water. Peter believed that if Jesus commanded him to walk on the water, then he could. So, when Peter had come down out of the boat, he walked on the water to go to Jesus. But when he saw that the wind *was* boisterous, he was afraid; and beginning to sink he cried out, saying, "Lord, save me!" (Matthew 14:30). Peter operated in faith, which is the reason why he was able to walk on the water.

However, as soon as he took his eyes off Jesus and focused on the storm, he began to sink. How many times do we do this when we compare ourselves to others? When we compare, we open ourselves up for discouragement, depression, and unbelief. You need to have tunnel vision for this faith walk. Focus your eyes on the One who is able to bless you. Keep your eyes on Jesus, not what you see.

Comparisons not only lead to discontentment and discouragement, but it also leads to jealousy, envy, and ungratefulness. God is constantly blessing us in other areas of our lives. We need to focus on those things instead of complaining and murmuring about the things we don't have yet. Once you start comparing your life to others', you open the door for jealousy and envy. You can become so consumed with jealousy and envy that you can't even be happy for your brothers and sisters in Christ. That's not the will of God. Every time you do this you allow the peace of God to escape you. God wants you to have peace in this season of your life. Learn to praise God for what He is already doing in your life. Praise Him in advance for your spouse. Worship Him in the secret place. Adore Him. I learned the hard way that comparing my life to others' would not change anything. It only made me a bitter person. After a while, I learned to adore the Lord. I learned to worship Him even with a broken heart. I learned to look around and thank God for every little thing. Sometimes I would pull over in an empty parking lot and just worship and be in His presence. I would thank Him for everything, even for those things that I desired in my heart that I did not have yet. I refused to grow bitter and not better. Be thankful and grateful for what God has already done for you. What parent would deny a grateful child a good gift? How much more will God in Heaven give to us who are grateful? The Bible says, "In everything give thanks; for this is the will of God in Christ Jesus for you." (1 Thessalonians 5:18). So, the will of God is clear. Stop comparing.

One of the many reasons we compare ourselves to others is because we want to please people. We want to look good for people. We want to project what we consider "perfect lives" to others. We want people to approve of our lives when God has already approved us. Paul in Galatians had the right mindset when he said, "Am I now trying to win the approval of human beings, or of God? Or am I trying to please people? If I were still trying to please people, I would not be a servant of Christ." (Gal. 1:10).

Don't worry about what people think about you. For a long time I didn't want to see or talk to anybody from my past because I dreaded them seeing me without a ring on my finger or even dating anyone. I was torturing myself. Since everyone else was married or had a significant other, I needed to have one, too—or so I thought. I was comparing my life to the lives of others and being consumed by what they thought of me. I've learned that there is no way you can be an effective servant of Christ while comparing yourself to other people. How can you sincerely take care of your home and marriage (which is a ministry) if you are constantly trying to keep up with "The Joneses"? Let your conduct be without covetousness; be content with such things as you have. For He Himself has said, "I will never leave you nor forsake you." (Hebrews 13:5).

Learn to keep your chin up and eyes on Jesus. He is not a God who will bless one and not the other. He is not a respecter of persons (Acts 10:34). For your own peace of mind, learn to be truly happy for those that God is blessing. Stop looking at everyone else and start looking at your Heavenly Father who is able to fulfill all your needs. Stay in faith and believe God will bless you at the appointed time. God's appointed time for your neighbor is not necessarily His appointed time for you.

Remember this: The Lord is not trying to make you feel bad by blessing others with the very desires of *your* heart. He is trying to mold you and build your confidence in Him, despite what it looks like. God will perfect those things that concern you. His mercy endures forever. He will not forsake the work of His hands (Psalm 138:8).

10

TEMPTATIONS

10

TEMPTATIONS

No temptation has overtaken you except such as is common to man; but God is faithful, who will not allow you to be tempted beyond what you are able, but with the temptation will also make the way of escape, that you may be able to bear it.

1 Corinthians 10:13

Many temptations will befall you as a single adult in Christ. Occasionally, you will be tempted to rush God. In those times, it may seem that you pray, fast, and obey God, but there's still no answer. The promise can seem nonexistent at times. Rushing God leads to the temptation to jump ahead of God. Some singles wait nearly 30-40 years on God for a spouse. When the weariness kicks in, some people jump ahead of God's timing and make decisions on their own. This also stems from the temptation to compromise. When it gets rough (and it will get rough) some begin to compromise their faith and beliefs. Compromising leads to the temptation to sin against God's Word in ways like sexual immorality and drunkenness.

Jesus was a single man. I'm convinced that He endured temptations just as we do today. He was God so He never sinned but He was still in this wretched flesh. Jesus was tempted when satan approached Him in the wilderness. He had been fasting 40 days and 40 nights. The Bible states that Jesus was hungry (Matthew 4). Of course, He was hungry! He was in human flesh! Of course, we want to have sex! We are in human flesh! We are mere mortals made for fellowship. We have natural, God-given desires. Therefore, there's nothing wrong with being tempted but we must overcome each temptation that satan throws our way. Jesus combated satan's every temptation with the Word of God (Matthew 4:1-11). I believe that the Word of God overrules flesh. We have to want to defeat sin. Some of us just give in and put out. However, that's not what God wants. We must be mature Christians that use the Word of God (our sword) to be victorious.

The enemy will try to distract you with many temptations, especially if you are trying to live a godly lifestyle. We must be privy to the devices of satan. Stay in the Word of God and use it to speak back to satan. You have power to overcome temptation. And if the temptation seems too much to bear, know that with the temptation God will also make the way of escape, so that you may be able to bear it (1 Corinthians 10:13).

The Bible says no temptation has overtaken you except such as common to man. Countless singles all over the world are enduring your same struggles. Nevertheless, God will not tempt us beyond our capacity. Do you really believe that God will not tempt us beyond our capacity? If so why do so many single Christians give in to temptations of various kinds? The Bible says that we are led astray by our own lusts (James 1:14). If we really want to wait on God, we will wait. If we really want to do our own thing then that's what we will eventually do. I can remember saying plenty of times, "Okay, God, this is it. I'm gonna wait on You." The next thing I knew I was manipulating my circumstances to have my own way. I recall a time when I called myself being celibate. I was really trying. However, when a childhood friend of mine anonymously named "Joe" came to visit me, all bets were off. I was really struggling about him coming over. But I thought to myself, *It will be harmless. No worries.* To make a long story short, I drank a considerable amount of wine and we had sex. I had disobeyed God. I had broken a promise I made to God because I was tired. I was tired of things not going my way and I was tired of waiting for sex. Therefore, I did what I really wanted to do instead of doing what was right. We all get weary sometimes. That does not give us the right to disrespect God in our conduct. As believers, we should live with respect for God. Furthermore, we have had human fathers who corrected *us,* and we paid *them* respect. Shall we not much more readily be in subjection to the Father of spirits and live? (Hebrews 12:9). I'm not saying it's easy to brush off temptation. It takes a lot of prayer, fasting, and faith to overcome temptation. You have to be determined to do the will of God.

On many occasions I wanted to tell God in a nasty tone, "Would You please just hurry up already?" I never said that aloud, but in my actions and in my heart I believe I did. The temptation to complain conquered me every time. I believe that when we complain, God is displeased and our wait becomes even longer. We have to learn to be patient with God that He may mature us. For you have need of endurance (patience) so that after you have done the will of God, you may receive the promise (Hebrews 10:36).

There were times when I was tempted to walk away from God. Life seemed unfair. I saw everybody else prospering and I thought, *This is a joke. I'm going my own way.* I was wrong. I've learned through my mistakes to continue to believe God. God is looking for people with passionate prayers about their desires. In The Book of Samuel Chapter 1, the Bible speaks of a woman named Hannah. She was desperate for God to change her circumstances. I'm sure she was tempted to quit and stop believing in God for her miracle. Instead Hannah went into the temple and prayed so passionately that the priest thought she was drunk. I love Hannah because she came to God desperate, bitter in soul, and in faith. Instead of giving in to the temptation to quit on God, she sought the Lord in prayer.

The Bible says that the Lord had shut up Hannah's womb (1 Samuel 1:6). I stated in the preface of this book that God is a God of purpose. Everything He does or does not do is on purpose. He shut up Hannah's womb on purpose; His purpose that His glory may be reveled in her circumstance. Hannah's son was the Prophet Samuel. He was the prophet to King Saul and King David. It was imperative that He was born at God's appointed time to carry out God's purposes. Had Hannah given up on the Living

God would we have had a Prophet Samuel from the womb of Hannah? God is still on the throne. God will answer your prayers according to His purpose. Now this is the confidence that we have in Him, that if we ask anything according to His will, He hears us. And if we know that He hears us, whatever we ask, we know that we have the petitions that we have asked of Him (1 John 5:14-15). Don't give in to the temptation to quit on God. Stay with Jesus.

Jesus is your help in the time of temptation. He understands exactly what you are dealing with. For in that He Himself has suffered, being tempted, He is able to aid those who are tempted (Hebrews 2:18). Don't allow your feelings, the world, or satan to lure you away from the Living God.

Be strong in the Lord [be empowered through your union with Him]; draw your strength from Him [that strength which His boundless might provides]. Put on God's whole armor [the armor of a heavy-armed soldier which God supplies], that you may be able successfully to stand up against [all] the strategies and the deceits of the devil.

For we are not wrestling with flesh and blood [contending only with physical opponents], but against the despotisms, against the powers, against [the master spirits who are] the world rulers of this present darkness, against the spirit forces of wickedness in the heavenly [supernatural] sphere. Therefore put on God's complete armor, that you may be able to resist and stand your ground on the evil day [of danger], and, having done all [the crisis demands], to stand [firmly in your place].

Stand therefore [hold your ground], having tightened the belt of truth around your loins and having put on the breastplate of integrity and of moral rectitude and right standing with God, and having shod your feet in preparation [to face the enemy with the firm-footed stability, the promptness, and the readiness produced by the good news] of the Gospel of peace. Lift up over all the [covering] shield of saving faith, upon which you can quench all the flaming missiles of the wicked [one].   (Ephesians   6:10-16).

11

GUARD YOUR HEART & YOUR THOUGHT LIFE

11

GUARD YOUR HEART & YOUR THOUGHT LIFE

*Keep your heart with all diligence; for out of it
spring the issues of life.*

Proverbs 4:23

The Bible consistently tells us to guard our hearts and minds. Whatever we think about or set our hearts on, that is what becomes magnified in our lives. If we meditate on the good, then good is visible. On the contrary, if we meditate on the bad, the bad will become magnified. For instance, if I wake up on the "wrong side of the bed" it is probably because I woke up concentrating on negative circumstances. Negativity will become evident in my facial expressions, my attitude, and ultimately, in my day. However, if I wake up grateful, speaking blessings into my day, expecting good things to happen, positivity will become evident in my day. We must be careful of what we think about and set our focus on. It must be done on purpose. It is a learned habit, but we must train ourselves to do it. Whatever is true, whatever is honorable, whatever is just, whatever is pure, whatever is lovely, whatever is commendable, if there is any excellence, if there is anything worthy of praise, think about these things (Philippians 4:8). God is commanding us to take our thoughts captive. The Lord knows that whatever we allow to enter our mind, ultimately will affect every area of our lives.

There is a saying that goes, "An idle mind is the devil's playground." This is so true. If we allow our minds to wander, the enemy will easily sneak in with tormenting thoughts. I am still learning to control my thoughts. There are moments when I have to remember the promises of God and proclaim that He is faithful. Isaiah 26:3 says, "You will guard him *and* keep him in perfect *and* constant peace whose mind [both its inclination and its character] is stayed on You, because he commits himself to You, leans on You, *and* hopes confidently in You." Learn to recite that scripture until it gets into your spirit. Allow that scripture to change your mind. If you allow your mind to drift, negative thoughts will creep in which will affect your faith. Doubt sets in because of negative thoughts. If you focus on not being married, never finding the "right one," and concentrating on everyone else's situations, then you will be depressed. Control what you think. You must think about what you are thinking about. If you are always thinking about an ex and how happy they are and how miserable you are, then you will continue to be miserable. Turn those negative thoughts into positive thoughts. You have the power to control your thought life.

For though we walk in the flesh, we do not war according to the flesh. For the weapons of our warfare *are* not carnal but mighty in God for pulling down strongholds, casting down arguments and every high thing that exalts itself against the knowledge of God, bringing every thought into captivity to the obedience of Christ, and being ready to punish all disobedience when your obedience is fulfilled (2 Corinthians 10:3-6). What is God saying to us here? Although we are in mortal, fleshly bodies, we don't wrestle with mortal, fleshly beings. We need to use the weapons that God has given us in order to keep our minds. We need to use them to pull down every stronghold (a wrongful thinking pattern based on deception and lies). Where do you think those deceptions and lies come from? They come from satan and our prior worldly and dysfunctional ways of living. We need to arm ourselves with the Word of God, constantly renewing our minds with the truth. When a negative thought comes into your mind, you can use the Word of God to bring that thought captive and make it obedient to Christ. You can cast down every argument and high thing that tries to exalt itself against the knowledge of God. When satan came to tempt Jesus in the wilderness, He used the Word of God to resist him, as we should. For example, the enemy will come to torment your mind and say things like, "It's been years. God hasn't answered you yet. It's never going to happen. If God were going to do it, He would have done it by now. Why are you still waiting?" When this happens, you can combat him with the truth and say, "For the LORD God *is* a sun and shield; The LORD will give grace and glory; No good *thing* will He withhold from those who walk uprightly (Psalm 84:11).

Furthermore, do you know that you have the mind of Christ? (Philippians 2:5 & 1 Corinthians 2:16). How amazing is that?! We don't have to wrestle with negative thoughts. The same spirit and mind that Jesus had when he walked the earth, is the same spirit and mind that we possess.

You're the only one who knows what you keep rehearsing in your mind. Only you know your imaginations. You must also be cautious of where you allow your mind to go. Your thoughts will cause you to sin against God. If you daydream about sex, then you will want to have sex. Just because you aren't actually doing it, doesn't mean you are not thinking about it. Your thoughts will cause you to masturbate if you think about sex long enough. Self-control is a fruit of the Spirit. Controlling your thoughts is an example of self-control. If you don't control your thoughts, you are leaving your mind vulnerable to attacks from the enemy. You must exercise self-control in your thought life.

Have you ever listened to a song so much that it was in your spirit when you woke up in the morning, driving in your car, and you rehearsed the song all day at work? That is what we need to do with the Word of God. We need to repeat the Word of God in our minds so that we will subconsciously rehearse it, leaving no room for the enemy the infiltrate our minds. What we watch on television, listen to on the radio, and hear other people say, all influence what we think. If you watch a movie with countless sex scenes, cursing, and ungodly behavior, you will eventually start to think on those things. If you hang around friends that are not waiting on God but are doing things their own way, and not filled with the Holy Spirit, then you will begin to think like those people. Please don't make the mistake of thinking that you are so spiritual that you can hang with ungodly people and it will not affect you. Bad company corrupts good character (1 Corinthians 15:33). Guarding your thought life also means guarding what you allow into your spirit from other people, not just satan.

Aside from guarding your mind, you must also guard your heart. A good man out of the good treasure of his heart brings forth good; and an evil man out of the evil treasure of his heart brings forth evil. For out of the abundance of the heart his mouth speaks (Luke 6:45). When a truthful person speaks, he or she speaks from the heart. The Bible says, death and life are in the power of the tongue, and they who indulge in it shall eat the fruit of it [for death or life] (Proverbs 18:21). Therefore, it is imperative that we guard our hearts. Whatever we speak, that is what will spring forth in our lives. Dare I say that some of the problems that we face are because we fail to tame our mouths? The way to spring forth life is to speak life.

Honestly, my heart only began to change as I spent more time in God's presence. The presence of God destroys the yolks of strongholds and transforms the hearts of man. There is no way you can be in the presence of God and not want to change. Change starts from the heart. We all know our issues, whether they be fear, lust, envy, jealousy, or a bad attitude, the real change must take place in the heart.

We should consistently check to make sure we are in right standing with God. The condition of your heart is vital to your walk with God. Furthermore, if your heart is in the wrong place, you will not be able to live victoriously in Christ as a single person. If you have evil desires in your heart you will act on those desires. However, if you allow God to change your heart you will soon have His desires. Delight yourself also in the Lord, and He will give you the desires *and* secret petitions of your heart (Psalm 37:4). You will begin to act on His desires, doing only what the Father wills. Set your mind to think the right things and allow God to change your heart as you meditate on His faithfulness.

12

TO DATE OR NOT TO DATE

12

TO DATE OR NOT TO DATE

*Desire without knowledge is not good, and
whoever makes haste with his feet misses his
way.*

Proverbs 19:2

Dating is a bit frustrating if you are doing
it God's way. If we are trying to live a godly
lifestyle we must always seek the will of God,
even in our dating lives. I don't believe there is
anything wrong with dating, but we must use
wisdom. We should seek God about whom to
date. I know some may say that this sounds
extreme. However, if you pray to God about
your financial needs, healing in your body, and
family crisis, why would you not pray to Him
about who you choose as a life partner? The
problem is that some people select what areas of
their lives they want to include God in. Then
when the areas they left Him out of become
disastrous, suddenly life is unfair. The Bible says
God stores up wisdom for the righteous; He is a

shield to us that walk uprightly (Proverbs 2:7). God wants the best for us. Seeking God in prayer and in His Word are sure ways to godly wisdom about whom you allow in your personal life. Without wisdom we fail to make wise choices. In the same way, without the Holy Spirit we are led astray.

Godly wisdom will keep you out of ungodly relationships, if you allow it. It will also save you from causing yourself heartache and grief. If we make decisions in our flesh, we'll end up dating anyone. This is not the will of God. Don't be so desperate that you fail to earnestly seek God about the person you are dating. Seeking God requires time in prayer (not just talking, but listening), seeking the scriptures for the will of God, and fasting. I can honestly say I now seek God about all my relationships with people, whether platonic or romantic. God is faithful. When I seek Him about a particular person, He answers. I always ask the Lord to show me the person for who they really are in the beginning of the relationship. That way if it's not from God, I can move on and save myself from the aggravation later. A word of advice: when God shows you the red flags or says, "No, this is not the one," you must be obedient and move on. That's the way wisdom works. You can have all the knowledge you want but it's what you do with that knowledge that makes you wise.

For a period of time God told me I was not to date. The Lord told me that it was sanctification time and that dating was a hindrance to what He wanted to do with me. I knew in my heart that He was right. Therefore, I stopped dating and focused on growing in the things of God. Deep down I knew my weaknesses just as God did. I knew that if I kept dating, eventually I would be tempted to fornicate, especially if I really liked the person. I was spiritual but I wasn't very strong yet. We must use wisdom even when it comes to ourselves. You know yourself better than anyone. Don't date if you can't control yourself. Eventually you will sin against God and cause another person to sin against God also. That is the last thing you want to do. If you are struggling with fornication, don't drag any one into your mess. Get before God and receive your deliverance.

Meditate on this: And whoever causes one of these little ones (these believers) who acknowledge *and* cleave to Me to stumble *and* sin, it would be better (more profitable and wholesome) for him if a [huge] millstone were hung about his neck, and he were thrown into the sea. And if your hand puts a stumbling block before you *and* causes you to sin, cut it off! It is more profitable *and* wholesome for you to go into life that is really worthwhile] maimed than with two hands to go to hell (Gehenna), into the fire that cannot be put out. And if your foot is a cause of stumbling *and* sin to you, cut it off! It is more profitable *and* wholesome for you to enter into life [that is really worthwhile] crippled than, having two feet, to be cast into hell (Gehenna). And if your eye causes you to stumble *and* sin, pluck it out! It is more profitable *and* wholesome for you to enter the kingdom of God with one eye than with two eyes to be thrown into hell (Gehenna). **Mark 9:42-47**

God is a God of purpose. We are people of purpose. If we are dating we should be dating with a purpose. Recreational dating can be hazardous. If you are dating because you are bored, lonely, or because it's just something to do to pass the time, you are not operating in wisdom. Recreational dating is not safe because there is no purpose in it. You are liable to fornicate and become emotionally attached to someone who is not the one whom God has in mind for you. We should be seeking God for the spouse He has for us, not dating randoms.

I believe that if we seek God in our dating lives we will be successful. I don't mean successful in a sense that you will have a spouse right away. I do mean that God will keep us from unhealthy relationships and lead us to the right person.

God has given me some precepts for dating that I like to call "The 10 Principles of Dating in Christ." I pray that these will help you in your decision-making.

THE 10 PRINCIPLES OF DATING IN CHRIST

1.   If the relationship does not glorify God, you shouldn't be in the relationship. If what you do together does not glorify God in any way, you need to either have a talk with the person or move on. In other words, if your relationship is not godly, you have a problem. We can be in fellowship with people and not even realize that God is not in it because we want it so badly. You both should be striving to please God. **Colossians 3:17 – And whatever you do [no matter what it is] in word or deed, do**

everything in the name of the Lord Jesus *and* in [dependence upon] His Person, giving praise to God the Father through Him.

2.   If the person leads you astray from the things of God, get away! Do not be misled: Bad company corrupts good character (1 Corinthians 15:33). In addition, if you find yourself constantly explaining and defending what you do for God that is a red flag. The person that God has for you will cheer you on in the things of God. You will not have to defend what you do for Christ. Furthermore, if you are dating someone that says he/she is a believer but the fruit is not there, something is wrong. You need to truly seek God about that person. They can be in church, sing, dance, and lead a homeless shelter, but the Fruit of the Spirit (Galatians Chapter 5) need to be evident. **1 Corinthians 5:11 - But now I am writing to you that you must not associate with anyone who claims to be a brother or sister but is sexually immoral or greedy, an idolater or slanderer, a drunkard or swindler. Do not even eat with such people**. I know many people will say, "Well, Jesus ate and drank with the sinners." Yes, He did. However, His purpose was ministry, not to hang out and get drunk.

3.   Don't be unequally yoked. Don't be with someone that is not of the same faith or an atheist. How can you believe God together? How can that person intercede on your behalf? I don't care how good-looking a person is; if they don't have the Spirit of God in them you need to leave them alone. If they are not operating under the power of the Holy Spirit, under what spirit are they operating? Unless God has confirmed that this person is for you and will come to salvation later, you need to consider moving on. **2 Corinthians 6:14-15 - Do not be yoked together with unbelievers. For what do righteousness and wickedness have in common? Or what fellowship can light have with darkness? What harmony is there between Christ and Belial? Or what does a believer have in common with an unbeliever?**

4.   If the relationship does not exemplify God's definition of love, it's not love. In my earlier relationships, I just knew that I understood what love was. Boy, was I wrong! As I grew in my relationship with Christ, He taught me what real love is. God is loving, patient, compassionate, and forgiving. His love is unconditional. It is not based on looks or status. He teaches us what love is by His actions towards us. As a result, we might love Him in

return, and love others unconditionally. **1 Corinthians 13:4-7 - Love endures long *and* is patient and kind; love never is envious *nor* boils over with jealousy, is not boastful *or* vainglorious, does not display itself haughtily. It is not conceited (arrogant and inflated with pride); it is not rude (unmannerly) *and* does not act unbecomingly. Love (God's love in us) does not insist on its own rights *or* its own way, *for* it is not self-seeking; it is not touchy *or* fretful *or* resentful; it takes no account of the evil done to it [it pays no attention to a suffered wrong]. It does not rejoice at injustice *and* unrighteousness, but rejoices when right *and* truth prevail. Love bears up under anything *and* everything that comes, is ever ready to believe the best of every person, its hopes are fadeless under all circumstances, and it endures everything [without weakening].**

5.   If you cannot remain sexually moral, don't date. Self-control is a Fruit of the Spirit. If you can't control yourself, maybe its best you don't date for a while. You have to be honest with yourself and with God. **Colossians 3:5 - So kill (deaden and deprive of power) the evil desire lurking in your members [those animal impulses and all that is earthly in you that is**

employed in sin]: sexual vice, impurity, sensual appetites, unholy desires, and all greed *and* covetousness, for that is idolatry (the deifying of self and other created things instead of God).

6.   If you don't see a future with the person, be honest and let that person go. You are hindering what God has for you. You are also keeping that person from what God has for them. **Proverbs 10:9 - Whoever walks in integrity walks securely, but whoever takes crooked paths will be found out.**

7.   If the relationship lacks trust, it's not healthy. Therefore, you need to rethink the relationship. I can remember being in a relationship where neither one of us trusted the other. It was pure torture. When two people don't trust each other, they are constantly living in a state of fear. There is no peace. Therefore, it is not of God. **1 John 4:18 - There is no fear in love; but perfect love casts out fear, because fear involves torment. But he who fears has not been made perfect in love.**

8.   The heart of the person is more important than the appearance. We all want someone who is considered attractive. Now, I know I'm not

perfect. I would hate for someone not to give me a chance because I don't meet his physical standards. Besides, charm is deceitful, and beauty is vain, but a woman who fears the Lord is to be praised (Proverbs 31:30). We should see people the way the Lord sees them. **1 Samuel 16:7 - But the LORD said to Samuel, "Do not look at his appearance or at his physical stature, because I have refused him. For *the* LORD *does* not *see* as man sees, for man looks at the outward appearance, but the LORD looks at the heart."**

9.   Introduce the person you are dating to your family and saved friends. Sometimes we are private when it comes to our dating lives. However, allowing those close to you (especially those with the spirit of discernment) will enable them to see things you can't see. When we are in love or really like a person, we are often blinded from the red flags. **1 John 4:1 - Beloved, do not believe every spirit, but test the spirits, whether they are of God...**

10.   Seek and utilize wisdom. Without wisdom, you will continue to make poor choices. Learn from your mistakes and seek God. **James 1:5 - If any of you lacks wisdom, you should**

ask God, who gives generously to all without finding fault, and it will be given to you.

I pray that this chapter helps you as you date according to God's will and purpose for your life. Remember to seek God about everything, even the things that seem minor. God cares for you.

13

BOUNDARIES IN DATING

13

BOUNDARIES IN DATING

*I therefore, the prisoner for the Lord, appeal to
and beg you to walk (lead a life) worthy of the
[divine] calling to which you have been called
[with behavior that is a credit to the summons to
God's service...*

Ephesians 4:1

As a Christian, you have a moral
responsibility to conduct yourself with integrity.
You are obligated to make sure that your
behavior is exemplary of a follower of Jesus
Christ. Therefore, in your dating life you must
set boundaries. You need boundaries to protect
yourself and the person you are dating.
Assuming that you are dating another believer,
you need to consider his or her integrity as well.
You'll want to make sure that you don't cause
them to stumble. Jesus said to his disciples,
"Things that cause people to stumble are bound
to come, but woe to anyone through whom they
come. It would be better for them to be thrown
into the sea with a millstone tied around their

neck than to cause one of these little ones to stumble (Luke 17:1-2).

When setting boundaries, a few things are simply common sense. Some decisions don't take prayer and fasting. Some decisions are a matter of right or wrong, wise or foolish. For instance, it's not wise be **alone** with someone you have strong feelings for on a regular basis. Temptation comes quickly when you spend time alone. Spending time together in group settings is helpful. Realistically, when dating, you want to spend quality "alone time" with the other person. However, the truth of the matter is you know your weaknesses. You know whether it is safe for you to be alone with this person or not. So, be wise, pray, and make decisions based on the Word of God. Additionally, other decisions, such as staying at their house late at night, sleeping over, and sleeping in the same bed, are not very wise. If you are trying to live a godly lifestyle, chances are these decisions will cause you to stumble.

We need to learn how to set boundaries when it comes to intimacy. Intimacy is the act of being intimate (i.e.; sharing private details of your life, revealing information about past sexual encounters, exposing deep emotional feelings, leaning on the person for emotional support, etc.)

SINGLE, SAVED, & SEEKING HIM

Boundaries are needed because dating does not guarantee marriage. Just because you are dating someone does not mean that God has intended for you to marry this person. You don't want to open yourself up to someone too soon and regret it later on. This can lead to unnecessary heartache. That's why it's important to seek God about whom to date. Thus, it is wise to use caution when being intimate while dating. Intimacy can be broken down in three categories: physical, emotional, and spiritual.

PHYSICAL INTIMACY

"It is good for a man not to have sexual relations with a woman." But since sexual immorality is occurring, each man should have sexual relations with his own wife, and each woman with her own husband (1 Corinthians 7:1-2). As the Apostle Paul explains this to the Ephesians, it is good for a husband and wife to have sex, not boyfriend and girlfriend. According to the Word of God, if you are not married you shouldn't be having sex. As previously stated, there are certain boundaries that you can set to avoid stumbling into sexual sin while dating. Foreplay, fondling, dry sex, and watching pornography are all surefire ways to lead you into sexual sin. I'll admit that abstaining from sex is one of the most difficult things to do. The desire to have sex is natural. However, God is a keeper (Jude 1:24). The key is, you have to want to be kept. God is not going to force you to live holy. You have to want it on your own. As a result, the Holy Spirit will enable you to live a holy life before God.

You need to pray and ask God to help you set boundaries in this area. You can't do it alone. You're going to need the Holy Spirit and the power of God to keep you. I'm telling you from personal experience. It is the grace of God that keeps me. It is because of His grace, His Holy Spirit, and power I am kept. Also, it would be wise to have friends in the faith to hold you accountable. You need people who are going to tell you the truth and rebuke you in love if necessary.

EMOTIONAL INTIMACY

Caution is definitely needed when becoming emotionally involved while dating. As I previously stated, dating in not a guarantee for marriage. You don't want to make the mistake of investing too much emotionally too soon.

Moreover, becoming emotionally intimate with this person may be dangerous if this person is your main source of emotional support. If this is not the person for you, this will lead to heartbreak and regret. While it is easy to become emotionally involved while dating, exercise wisdom and set boundaries. If you're not sure, pray and ask God how much you should share with this person. The Bible says in James 1:5, "If any of you lacks wisdom, let him ask of God, who gives to all liberally and without reproach, and it will be given to him."

You must learn to keep *and* guard your heart with all vigilance *and* above all that you guard, for out of it flow the springs of life (Proverbs 4:23). I'm not saying build up walls so the person can't get in. Just be mindful of what you expose your heart to, for out of it flow the springs of life. In other words, out of your heart flow the issues of life. Be careful about what and whom you allow into your heart. In most cases, you can avoid hurting others and being hurt by guarding your heart.

SPIRITUAL INTIMACY

Boundaries for spiritual intimacy are needed as well. Many married couples practice prayer, devotion, and worship together. Most of the time people that are dating do the same. In this way, it's easy to develop spiritual intimacy with people of the same faith. One minute you're sharing personal testimonies, then prayer, and before you know it you've started an intimate spiritual relationship with this person. However, the Bible tells us to test the spirits to see whether they are from God (1 John 4:1). Seek God about who you should pray with and open yourself up to spiritually. You need to set some boundaries in your spiritual life. It would be awful if you've let this person in without using wisdom.

I know this chapter may seem a bit "too saved." However, God tells us in Proverbs 16:3, to roll our works upon the Lord [commit and trust them wholly to Him; He will cause our thoughts to become agreeable to His will, and] so shall our plans be established *and* succeed. I believe the Word of God. We can apply the Word of God to every aspect of our lives, even dating. God is concerned about every area of our lives. I want to encourage you to set boundaries in your dating and seek God about every person you even think about dating. Proverbs 19:2 says, "Desire without knowledge is not good, and to be overhasty is to sin *and* miss the mark. Don't miss the mark by acting hastily without seeking God first.

14
S.E.X.

14

S.E.X.

Or do you not know that your body is the temple of the Holy Spirit who is in you, whom you have from God, and you are not your own? For you were bought at a price; therefore glorify God in your body and in your spirit, which are God's.

1 Corinthians 6:19-20

Every good and perfect gift is from above, coming down from the Father of lights with whom there is no variation or shadow due to change (James 1:17). Sex is a good and perfect gift from God. It should be enjoyed, between a man and a woman, a husband and a wife. Contrarily, according the ways of the world and modern society, anything goes. The world says we can have sex carelessly with whomever we want. Moral boundaries are uncommon in today's society. Scoffers may say that if God intended us to be celibate, why would He make it so difficult for us? Unbelievers may say sex is natural and we shouldn't have to wait until we are married.

Honestly, I felt the same way before my mind was changed by the Holy Spirit. Before I understood who I am in Christ, I did whatever I wanted. I slept with whomever I wanted and it didn't bother me. This erroneous way of thinking (stronghold) went on for years. I didn't know Christ and neither did anyone with whom I associated myself. Therefore, I thought sex with your boyfriend or girlfriend was natural and okay. Even when my attendance in church began to increase, this stronghold was still active. I knew it was wrong but that wasn't enough to make me stop. This was because authentic repentance had not taken place yet. My mind had not yet changed. Some people go to church every Sunday, Tuesday, Wednesday, and Friday night. They are in almost every ministry, and they can quote the Bible backwards. Unfortunately, the demonic strongholds in their lives have not been broken. Those same people think it's okay to have sex with whomever they want whenever they want. This was the mentality I had. It wasn't until I began to cooperate with the Holy Spirit that I did a complete 180. The Holy Spirit and the Word of God began to change my mind. I became aware that I was giving away

SINGLE, SAVED, & SEEKING HIM

something that should be treasured: my body. Fornication was an inconsistency that God had to break from my life. When the Holy Spirit began to change my mind, I realized that by fornicating I was opening myself up to the possibility of transferring spirits, emotional damage, diseases, and unwanted pregnancies. At that point, I honestly didn't want anyone else touching me except my future husband. I believe in my heart that this is what God wanted as well.

In today's society, principles such as keeping one's self for marriage or living your life with reverence for God is abnormal. Do not be conformed to this world, but be transformed by the renewing of your mind, that you may prove what is that good and acceptable and perfect will of God (Romans 12:2). The renewing of the mind starts with the Word of God. We must renew our minds daily with the Word of God. It is a consistent cleansing and it will transform your way of thinking. Be renewed. For this is the will of God, that you should be consecrated (separated and set apart for pure and holy living): that you should abstain and shrink from all sexual vice, that each one of you should know how to possess (control and manage) his own body in consecration (purity, separated from things profane) and honor, not [to be used] in the passion of lust like the heathen, who are ignorant of the true God and have no knowledge of His will (1 Thessalonians 4:3-5).

If you are reading this book, I pray that you have some form of a relationship with Jesus Christ. If you do, you already know that sexual immorality is not pleasing in God's sight. We must remain abstinent while we are single. I'll be the first to raise my hand to say it's one of the most difficult tasks I've ever faced in my life. To abstain from sex requires much prayer, fasting, and trusting God. You will fail at times. Yet at some point you must get serious about your walk with God. If you cannot control your sexual desires, Apostle Paul advises, "But to the unmarried people and to the widows, I declare that it is well (good, advantageous, expedient, and wholesome) for them to remain [single] even as I do. But if they have not self-control (restraint of their passions), they should marry. For it is better to marry than to be aflame [with passion and tortured continually with ungratified desire]." (1 Corinthians 7:8-9).

Don't continue to live willfully in sin. Do you not know that the unrighteous will not inherit the kingdom of God? Do not be deceived. Neither fornicators, nor idolaters, nor adulterers, nor homosexuals, nor sodomites (1 Corinthians 6:9). God is calling His people to a higher standard of living. Yes, God is gracious. He is faithful and just to forgive us of our sins if we confess them (1 John 1:9). That doesn't mean that we should take advantage of God's grace and mercy. Make no mistake about it, He loves us, but He's no pushover. Do not be deceived. God is not mocked; for whatever a man sows, that he will also reap. For he who sows to his flesh will of the flesh reap corruption, but he who sows to the Spirit will of the Spirit reap everlasting life (Galatians 6:7-8). What you think no one sees, He sees. What you think is okay to do in the dark, God will show you that it's not in the light. Don't wait for God to expose you. Spare yourself the embarrassment and turn from your sins.

I believe that sometimes people fail to understand the repercussions of unsolicited sex. The danger of sexually transmitted diseases, the emotional attachments that come with sex, unplanned pregnancies, and the spirits that we allow to attach themselves to us by the very act of sex are all repercussions that can affect our lives forever. Another factor that caused me to turn from fornication was the fact that I became one with every person I slept with. That person you slept with may not have a sexually transmitted disease, but could be wrestling with demonic spirits that you just allowed to transfer to you, all because you were tired of waiting on God. Can you imagine? **Do you not know that your bodies are members of Christ? Shall I then take the members of Christ and make *them* members of a harlot? Certainly not! Or do you not know that he who is joined to a harlot is one body *with her?* For "the two," He says, "shall become one flesh." But he who is joined to the Lord is one spirit *with Him.* (**1 Corinthians 6:15-17). I knows it's easier said than done, but join yourself to the One Who is able to do exceedingly abundantly above all that we ask or think, according to the power that works in us (Ephesians 3:20).

Those of us in Christ are a holy set apart people. We are a chosen race, a royal priesthood, a dedicated nation, [God's] own purchased, special people, that we may set forth the wonderful deeds *and* display the virtues and perfections of Him Who called us out of darkness into His marvelous light (1 Peter 2:9). How can we display the virtues and perfections of Him Who called us out of darkness if we are still fumbling around in the darkness? We are to be pure in our conduct even in today's society.

We should also strive for purity in our thought life. The Bible says whoever looks at a woman to lust for her has already committed adultery with her in his heart. Sin starts in the mind first and brings forth what is in your heart. Learn to renew your mind and guard your thought life. Remember, without holiness no man shall see God (Hebrews 12:14).

MASTURBATION

Yes, the big "M" word! Let's talk about it. Of course many will say there is nothing wrong with self-pleasure. I can remember thinking, *Well, Lord, if I can't get my pleasure that way, I'll try this way.* I was never a big fan of masturbation but as time progressed and there were still no prospects for marriage I thought, *Why not?* If the Holy Spirit lives inside of us, that means that God's Spirit is always present. How can you be so bold to masturbate knowing that God is present? We are to glorify God with our bodies. We are to be living sacrifices. Flee sexual immorality. Every sin that a man does is outside the body, but he who commits sexual immorality sins against his own body (1 Corinthians 6:18). Your body is the sanctuary for the Holy Spirit. I can remember when God said to me, "Walk before me, and be thou perfect." Someone told me to look it up in the Bible and so I did.

In Genesis 17, God was speaking to Abraham and He said, "I am the Almighty God; walk before me, and be thou perfect." God was telling me to live my life before Him as if we are face to face. He was telling me that I should know in my heart that He is always present and watching me. I understood what God was saying to me, which made it pretty uncomfortable to masturbate any longer. I know this is a touchy subject and it is difficult to accomplish, but God is our Keeper. He will keep you if you want to be kept. Furthermore, if we are doing things that we are ashamed of, chances are we shouldn't be doing it. I advise you to walk before God and be thou perfect. The Holy Spirit will help you. And do not present your members *as* instruments of unrighteousness to sin, but present yourselves to God as being alive from the dead, and your members *as* instruments of righteousness to God (Romans 6:13).

SEXUAL INTEGRITY

The Lord showed me something about His servant Joseph. His integrity and reverence for God was authentic. Joseph was a slave. He was sold into slavery by his own family. If he wanted to be bitter and live with disregard for God's standards he could have. I'm sure to many people this behavior would have made sense. However, Joseph chose to be a man of integrity. **Now Joseph was an attractive person and fine looking. Then after a time his master's wife cast her eyes upon Joseph, and she said, "Lie with me."** However, he refused and said to his master's wife, "See here, with me in the house my master has concern about nothing; he has put all that he has in my care. He is not greater in this house than I am; nor has he kept anything from me except you, for you are his wife. How then can I do this great evil and sin against God?"** (Genesis 39:6-9) God didn't bless Joseph with a spouse until later on in his life. I'm sure as a grown man he was tempted to sleep with this woman. Despite this fact and all the hardships he endured, his main concern was not doing evil and sinning against God. God is looking for people who reverence Him. He is looking for those who will stand for righteousness despite what society says. Joseph loved and respected God so much that He didn't want to displease Him. He fled from this woman so fast that his cloak was pulled off his body (Genesis 39:13). When was the last time you fled sexual sin this fast? Where can God find men and women with such integrity? Are you one of those God is looking for? For God did not call us to uncleanness, but in holiness (1 Thessalonians 4:7).

Food [is intended] for the stomach and the stomach for food, but God will finally end [the functions of] both *and* bring them to nothing. The body is not intended for sexual immorality, but [is intended] for the Lord, and the Lord [is intended] for the body [to save, sanctify, and raise it again]. (1 Corinthians 6:13)

Besides waiting on God, I believe sexual purity is the hardest task to fulfill in Christ. However, I'm convinced that God is able to continue to keep you and I. Be steadfast in the Lord. Pray constantly. Ask the Lord to help you to stay pure. Allow Him to be God in your life. Know that His statutes are for our blessing, not hindrance.

15

FAITH OVER FEELINGS

15

FAITH OVER FEELINGS

But without faith it is impossible to please Him,
for he who comes to God must believe that He is,
and that He is a rewarder of those who diligently
seek Him.

Hebrews 11:6

God gave us emotions. There is nothing wrong with feeling a certain way about a situation. If you are sad, then be sad. If you are happy, then be happy. However, it is not God's intention for us to allow our feelings to rule over us. Many times throughout my journey as a single Christian, I have allowed my feelings to override my faith. Between the sting of loneliness and my disappointment with God's timing, I began to lose hope at times. Some days I was content. Other days I felt like I wanted to curl up and die. My emotions were all over the place. They were unstable. Knowing this, I knew that I could not trust my feelings. I knew that the one thing that I could trust was the Word of God.

For the Word of the LORD is right and true; He is faithful in all He does (Psalms 33:4).

The Bible tells us that God is faithful (1 Corinthians 1:9). This means that He is trustworthy. Since God is His Word (John 1:1), then we can trust His every word. How do we know that God is His Word? The Bible tells us that God the Father and Jesus Christ the Son are one (John 10:30). If God is His Son, who is the Living Word, then we know that God is His Word. Therefore, we can trust what the Bible says about God. No matter how you feel, believe that God is faithful to perform His Word. God is touched by your emotions, but they don't move Him. He acts according to your faith.

Despite the truth, I chose my feelings over faith. I can remember countless Sunday mornings when I did not "feel" like going to church. I "felt" like it was a waste of time. I thought, *Go to church and then what? Come back home to the same situation? Why am I continuously seeking God? It doesn't pay off so I'm not going.* Likewise, I allowed my emotions to keep me from my ministry duties. I was tired of pouring out and seeing no results. I'm not just talking about ministry duties in church. Ministry starts at home with family. Sometimes I would fail to do what God was calling me to do in my own family because I became weary in well-doing. God desires to use people that He can trust. God needs to know that we will remain faithful out of season. I can remember going out to my car on my lunch breaks to pray only to end up in tears because I "felt" as if God had forgotten about me. I would go days without praying because I thought, *What's the point? People are living their lives how they please and they seem more blessed than I am. So why seek God?* I was angry, disappointed, weary, and frustrated all at the same time, most of the time. I allowed my feelings to negate the truth about God's faithful character.

In Hebrews 11:6, the end of the verse says, "...for he who comes to God **must believe** that He is, and **that He is a rewarder of those who diligently seek Him.**" The truth of the matter is God does reward those who diligently seek Him. We diligently seek Him because we have faith that He will reward us. One of the biggest tactics that the enemy uses is to use our own feelings against us. If he can get you stop seeking God by faith, then he knows that you will never receive anything from God because we receive the promises of God by faith. Furthermore, the scripture says, "But without faith it is impossible to please God..." I was consumed with doing the right things and being right when all God wanted me to do was live by faith. How could I please God if I didn't have faith that He would make good on His promises? Why would God bless me for diligently seeking Him if I didn't even believe that He would? Instead of saying, "Why go to church or pray?" I began to say, "I'm going to keep going to church and praying because I know that God is a rewarder of those who diligently seek Him. God will reward me." That's how you use the Word of God to activate the promises of God in your life. Moreover, that's how you defeat the enemy's lies—with the Word of God.

I realize that many times when I allowed my feelings to keep me from the house of God, I missed out. Faith comes by hearing, and hearing by the Word of God (Romans 10:17). The faith lift that I needed was not at home sulking in my bed, but it was in the house of God. Yes, we can always turn on the television or laptop to get a quick word. Nevertheless, there is nothing like being in God's house with like-minded people in the holy presence of a holy God. The presence of God Himself will make you grateful, joyful, hopeful, and free. When you are in the presence of God you can let those negative feelings go. You can release them to Him.

One of my outlets that I was and still am consistent in is the intercessory prayer group at my church. There is something special about the sanctuary at 8 AM on a Sunday morning when no one else is there. I'm free to worship, cry, and pray as freely as I want. Worship is a great way to overcome your feelings. Worship takes you to another dimension. It compels you to push past your feelings and acknowledge God for who He is. Worship ushers in the presence of God. Worship is the key to overcoming those negative feelings. Don't get me wrong. There were times when I was too disappointed with God to worship Him. The disappointment made me so angry that I couldn't even open my mouth. However, we're talking about God Almighty. The One who placed the sun, moon, and the stars in their places. The One who split the Red Sea. The One who continuously delivers us from all of our troubles. The One who sent His Son to die for our sins. The One who has given us eternal life. How can we not worship Him?

I know it's difficult at times to have faith despite what you're feeling. What you see can make you feel sad all day long if you let it. Nevertheless, we, the just (justified by Christ's blood) are called to live by faith, not by sight (2 Corinthians 5:7). We have to remember that what we see is temporal, but what we don't see (the promises of God) are eternal. Faith goes beyond what you feel. Now faith is the substance of things hoped for, the evidence of things not seen (Hebrews 11:1). I encourage you to focus on the following scriptures. Be encouraged.

2 Corinthians 4:7-9 - But we have this treasure in earthen vessels, that the excellence of the power may be of God and not of us. *We are* hard-pressed on every side, yet not crushed; *we are* perplexed, but not in despair; persecuted, but not forsaken; struck down, but not destroyed.

2 Corinthians 4:13 - And since we have the same spirit of faith, according to what is written, "I believed and therefore I spoke," we also believe and therefore speak.

2 Corinthians 4:16-18 - Therefore we do not lose heart. Even though our outward *man* is perishing, yet the inward man is being renewed day by day. For our light affliction, which is but for a moment, is working for us a far more exceeding *and* eternal weight of glory, while we do not look at the things which are seen, but at the things which are not seen. For the things which are seen *are* temporary, but the things which *are* not seen are eternal.

Romans 4:20-21 - No unbelief *or* distrust made him waver (doubtingly question) concerning the promise of God, but he grew strong *and* was empowered by faith as he gave praise *and* glory to God, fully satisfied *and* assured that God was able *and* mighty to keep His word *and* to do what He had promised.

Mark 11:22-24 - So Jesus answered and said to them, "Have faith in God. For assuredly, I say to you, whoever says to this mountain, 'Be removed and be cast into the sea,' and does not doubt in his heart, but believes that those things he says will be done, he will have whatever he says. Therefore I say to you, whatever things you ask when you pray, believe that you receive *them,* and you will have *them.*

Luke 1:37 - For with God nothing is ever impossible *and* no word from God shall be without power *or* impossible of fulfillment.

16

THE IDOL OF MARRIAGE

16

THE IDOL OF MARRIAGE

And the Word of the Lord came to me, saying,
"Son of man, these men have set up their idols in
their hearts, and put before them that which
causes them to stumble into iniquity. Should I let
Myself be inquired of at all by them?

Ezekiel 14:2-3

There is nothing wrong with the desire for a godly marriage. I believe that it is a God-given desire because many people desire marriage, but not everyone desires a godly marriage. God created marriage, so it is good. For everything God has created is good, and nothing is to be thrown away or refused if it is received with thanksgiving. For it is hallowed and consecrated by the Word of God and by prayer (1 Timothy 4:4-5). Therefore, your desire for a godly marriage is good in the eyes of God. It is good to pray and believe God for it. Surely,

He can perform it for you. The problem arises when we begin to idolize marriage. When the desire for the created becomes greater than the desire for the Creator, it becomes idolatry.

To understand how marriage becomes an idol, let us first define idolatry according to God's Word. Many times when God spoke of idols, He described carved images, golden statues, cast metal, etc. **"You shall have no other gods before Me. You shall not make for yourself a carved image—any likeness of anything that is in Heaven above, or that is in the earth beneath, or that is in the water under the earth; you shall not bow down to them nor serve them. For I, the Lord your God, am a jealous God, visiting the iniquity of the fathers upon the children to the third and fourth generations of those who hate Me." (Ex. 20:3-5).** These idols were man-made images that people worshipped, prayed to, and regarded higher than God Himself. They trusted these false gods rather than trust the one true God. However, in Ezekiel 14:2-3, God speaks about how the elders in Israel set up their idols in their hearts, and put before them that which caused them to stumble into iniquity. He said to the Prophet Ezekiel, "Should I let Myself be inquired of at all by them?" In other words,

SINGLE, SAVED, & SEEKING HIM

"Should I even regard their prayers?" God was frustrated with these people because they had allowed the idols in their hearts to cause them to stumble into iniquity. Iniquity means immorality or sin. An idol is any person or thing that you allow to draw you away from the ways and will God. Therefore, when you allow a person or thing to lead you astray from the ways and will of God, it is idolatry. When you regard a person or thing higher than God, it is idolatry.

It is not the will of God that you desire marriage more than you desire Him. Neither is it the will of God that you desire a person more than you desire His presence. I remember dating a certain fellow a few years back. I was still a babe in Christ but I knew in my heart that we were not meant to be together. When I was with him, I rarely wanted to go to church, we frequently had sex, and I was living in disobedience to God. When I was with him, I wanted to do everything I knew I should not do. Looking back, I now know that it was idolatry. I was allowing this relationship to keep me from the ways and will of God. It was and is God's will that I go higher in the things of God. However, God knew that if I continued in that relationship, it would not happen. I don't blame the guy because God was always speaking to me about it throughout the years. However, I consistently put this person before God. I wanted to be in a relationship with a man more than I wanted to be in a relationship with Almighty God. I desired this guy more than I desired the presence of God. The Lord had to break that relationship and break me out of that destructive behavioral pattern.

God is not the kind of God that will allow you to love a person more than you love Him. God is a jealous God (Deuteronomy 6:15). Yes, it's good to love one another; Jesus commands this (Mark 12:31). Yet, Christ desires people that are willing to lay down their lives for Him. He is looking for disciples that are willing to give up everything to follow Him. You have to be willing to love God more than you love your spouse. Jesus says, "If anyone comes to Me and does not hate his [own] father and mother in the sense of indifference to or relative disregard for them in comparison with his attitude toward God] and [likewise] his wife and children and brothers and sisters—[yes] and even his own life also—he cannot be My disciple." (Luke 14:26). I'm reminded of Abraham, as he was willing to sacrifice his only son in obedience to God's command (Genesis 22). Also, Hannah, in her barrenness, prayed to the Lord for a child (1

Samuel 1). God answered her prayer yet she committed that child to the Lord. As much as we desire marriage, we have to be willing to commit that marriage or person to the Lord should He ask. We must be willing to love God more than that relationship. Until you get to that place, God may delay your request. You must have a heart after God, not His blessings.

Some relationships are not healthy for us. Most of the time we know when they aren't, but we continue in them anyway. When we allow relationships to cause us to stumble, it becomes detrimental to our walk with God. Many people are so desperate for marriage and/or companionship that they are willing to compromise their integrity to obtain it. They allow the desire to cause them to stumble into iniquity. As Paul says, "But fornication and all uncleanness or covetousness, let it not even be named among you, as is fitting for saints; neither filthiness, nor foolish talking, nor coarse jesting, which are not fitting, but rather giving of thanks. For this you know, that no fornicator, unclean person, nor covetous man, who is an idolater, has any inheritance in the kingdom of Christ and God." (Ephesians 5:3-5). Don't become so obsessed with the desire to be married that you forsake the ways of God. Honestly, why would you want to be with anyone that encourages you to stray from the things of God? Sometimes we can want something so much that it can cause us to do things that are contrary to the will of God. I can remember wanting companionship so badly that I would keep company with guys I knew couldn't care less about God. I didn't care. I wanted to be with someone. The desire for male companionship was greater for my desire for God. Our desire for God should be our greatest heart's desire.

Those who pay regard to false, useless, *and* worthless idols forsake their own [Source of] mercy *and* loving-kindness (Jonah 2:8). This verse speaks volumes. God is our Source for everything we need. When we regard people or things more highly than our true Source, we forsake our own mercy and loving kindness. Your husband, wife, or fiancé is not your source. God is your Source. We need to understand and know that before we enter into any courtship or marriage. Marriage is honorable in God's sight, but He will not allow you to honor your spouse over Him. Husbands and wives are to submit to one another as Christ commanded, but not the point of forsaking the ways of God. He knows our hearts. Some people are still waiting on the promise of marriage because God knows that some will forsake Him after the blessing. I urge you to get before the Lord and ask Him to give you a deeper desire for Him. Ask Him to help you to remember Him, even after you fall in love with the one He is sending you for marriage. Don't forget your Source. The Bible says in Deuteronomy 8:19, **"Then it shall be, if you by any means forget the LORD your God, and follow other gods, and serve them and worship them, I testify against you this day that you shall surely perish."** God knows who will forget Him after the blessing. He knows who will perish. Your heart must be fixed on Jesus even after the spouse comes.

Every good and every perfect gift is from above, and comes down from the Father of lights, with whom there is no variation or shadow of turning (James 1:17). Your marriage, your children, and your future are all good and perfect gifts from God above. Don't make the mistake of allowing your gifts to take the place of your Father in Heaven. Desire what is good, but desire God even more.

17
THE SHAME OF IT ALL

17

THE SHAME OF IT ALL

The Scripture says, No man who believes in Him
[who adheres to, relies on, and trusts in Him]
will [ever] be put to shame or be disappointed.

Romans 10:11

Romans 10:11 is what I like to call a "hold on" scripture. Every now and again, you need a promise from God to hold on to no matter what it looks like. As you are single, there will be times where it seems God has forgotten you. There may also be times where you may feel embarrassed about your singlesness. Nevertheless, take heart and know that no man who believes in Him will ever be put to shame or disappointed. Continue to trust God.

Every holiday season, wedding, bridal shower, baby shower, I would have to prepare myself. I would have to prepare myself for questions and comments such as, "When are you getting married? What are you waiting for?

You'd better hurry up." I would have to prepare my heart and mind because I knew that satan was ready to send those negative thoughts and feelings. Honestly, there were times when I thought, *God where are you? You promised. This is getting a bit embarrassing.* The longer the wait and the older you get, the more embarrassed you may feel, especially in those particular times of the year. It can be rough as you watch all of your friends and even younger siblings get married while you are still waiting on God. At one point, it was difficult for me to watch unsaved people get married and have their happily ever after while I continued to wait on God. Nevertheless, the Bible says, be still *and* rest in the Lord; wait for Him *and* patiently lean yourself upon Him; fret not yourself because of him who prospers in his way, because of the man who brings wicked devices to pass (Psalm 37:7). It was also embarrassing to see ex-boyfriends get married while I remained single (still waiting on God). Sometimes it can feel as if God has forgotten us or that He is too busy blessing everyone else. However, David reminds us of God's faithfulness in Psalm 37:25, he says, "I have been young and now am old, yet have I not seen the [uncompromisingly] righteous forsaken or their seed begging bread." God is faithful. He will hear and answer.

As I was writing this chapter, the Lord lead me to Hebrews 12, which talks about fixing our eyes on Jesus that we may run the race that is set before us. This is the race of faith. Looking to Jesus, the Founder and Perfecter of our faith, who for the joy that was set before him endured the cross, despising the shame, and is seated at the right hand of the throne of God (Hebrews 12:2). I love the Amplified Version, which translates, Looking away [from all that will distract] to Jesus, Who is the Leader *and* the Source of our faith [giving the first incentive for our belief] and is also it's Finisher [bringing it to maturity and perfection]. He, for the joy [of obtaining the prize] that was set before Him, endured the cross, despising *and* ignoring the shame, and is now seated at the right hand of the throne of God (Hebrews12:2). No matter how much shame or embarrassment you may feel, you are to fix your eyes on Jesus. Jesus is our example of how we are to go through trials. Think of how embarrassed Jesus must have felt to believe God despite His sufferings. He was beaten, tortured, and nailed to the cross for all to see. More than that, they mocked him. Even in this, He ignored the shame and pain for the prize that was set before Him. No matter how bad it gets, we must keep in mind the prize that is set before us. We have the promise of eternal life and we are to emulate Christ in all things. We are to remember that God knows the plans He has for us. It is a plan for good and not of evil, to give us hope and a future. God wants to give us an expected end—His expected end.

You need to persevere in this season of your life. You must be patient with God and His timing. You may have been waiting on God for what seems a lifetime. Others may be going before you getting married and having babies. All of this may seem a bit shameful to you as you continue to trust God. However, the Bible says, "My brethren, take the prophets, who spoke in the name of the Lord, as an example of suffering and patience. Indeed, we count them blessed who endure. You have heard of the perseverance of Job and seen the end *intended by* the Lord—that the Lord is very compassionate and merciful." (James 5:10-11). Job suffered and endured in that particular season of His life. He waited on God for his change. When it was all over, Job was even more blessed after he went through trusting the Lord.

I too have felt embarrassed and ashamed in this season of my life. However, I'm convinced that God knows very well what He is doing. I'm convinced that He is able and will bless me at the appointed time. You may be suffering now but it is good to suffer for doing the right thing. Don't be like everyone else and decide you are going to do things your way because you are tired of the embarrassment. **For this is a gracious thing, when, mindful of God, one endures sorrows while suffering unjustly. For what credit is it if, when you sin and are beaten for it, you endure? But if when you do good and suffer for it you endure, this is a gracious thing in the sight of God. For to this you have been called, because Christ also suffered for you, leaving you an example, so that you might follow in his steps (1 Peter 2:19-21, ESV).**

Remember: Blessed is the one who perseveres under trial because, having stood the test, that person will receive the crown of life that the Lord has promised to those who love him (James 1:12).

18

LEARNING
CONTENTMENT

18

LEARNING CONTENTMENT

*Not that I am implying that I was in any personal
want, for I have learned how to be content
(satisfied to the point where I am not disturbed
or disquieted) in whatever state I am. I know
how to be abased and live humbly in straitened
circumstances, and I know also how to enjoy
plenty and live in abundance. I have learned in
any and all circumstances the secret of facing
every situation, whether well-fed or going
hungry, having a sufficiency and enough to spare
or going without and being in want.*

Philippians 4:11-12

There is one word that Paul used in the
preceding scripture that grips my attention. In
regard to contentment, he said, "I have **learned**,"
which means it wasn't immediate. Contentment
is learned. It takes time and is a process. Paul
explains in Philippians that through everything

he experienced, he learned how to be content. Numerous moments I've thought to myself, *How can I be content when I feel like my dreams and desires are delayed? How can I have peace knowing that the desires of my heart are unfulfilled?* As I looked at the life of the Apostle Paul, it boggled my mind how this man could say he had contentment. The amplified version of Philippians 4:11 explains how the word content in this verse means he was satisfied to the point where he was not disturbed or disquieted. He was at peace in every circumstance. Paul says in 2 Corinthians 11:24-27, "Five times I received from the Jews the forty lashes minus one. Three times I was beaten with rods, once I was pelted with stones, three times I was shipwrecked, I spent a night and a day in the open sea, I have been constantly on the move. I have been in danger from rivers, in danger from bandits, in danger from my fellow Jews, in danger from Gentiles; in danger in the city, in danger in the country, in danger at sea; and in danger from false believers. I have labored and toiled and have often gone without sleep; I have known hunger and thirst and have often gone without food; I have been cold and naked." Nevertheless, he learned contentment in those situations by remaining in Jesus Christ. He says, "I can do all this through Him who gives me strength." (Phil. 4:13).

Everything that could have possibly gone wrong for Paul went wrong. However, he learned contentment. Sometimes God will allow us to experience those moments when everyone else around us being blessed with marriage proposals, babies, and a new beginning. He may allow us to experience loneliness and heartache to show us that His grace is sufficient (2 Corin. 12:9). He wants us to learn contentment even in the worst situations. It is easy to be content when life is perfect and you have everything your heart desires. However, we are a set apart people. While some people in the world may settle for less just to have companionship or lose their minds because they don't have a spouse, we who are God's chosen learn contentment in Him. I've often felt a discomfort as I continued to wait on the Lord for the next phase of my life to begin. It seemed so far off. Everything around me told me that I would not get married and that God had forgotten about me. Those negative feelings overtook me because I was in my flesh. I could not experience contentment because I was living by sight, not by faith.

As I stated earlier, contentment is learned. Moreover, it is not learned overnight.

Although it may not be what you want or expected, God is using this season to perfect you. In the midst of perfecting you He is teaching you how to be content in every circumstance, whether married or single. Throughout this life God is going to allow you to go through a series of testing. It is for the perfecting of your faith. **These have come so that the proven genuineness of your faith—of greater worth than gold, which perishes even though refined by fire—may result in praise, glory and honor when Jesus Christ is revealed (1 Peter 1:7).** Be content in knowing that He is at work in you, even in this season. As singles in Christ we need to know that contentment is attainable. It is by the Spirit of God that we receive supernatural strength to endure all things. When all hope seems lost and there are no prospects for marriage, God is still an able God. His grace is certainly sufficient. He is able to keep your mind and your emotions, but you must remain in Him. You can choose to fight God in this season or to trust Him. Believe that He will answer your prayers in His good time, and learn contentment. A peace comes from trusting God. When you know and believe that God is going to perform the impossible, contentment rests on you. Don't fret yourself because of what you are going through. God is a keeper. He will keep you in perfect peace as you keep your mind stayed on Him (Isaiah 26:3).

I know that I mention Joseph a lot, however there is a scripture in the Bible that assures me that he also was content, even after all he suffered. This is a man who was sold into slavery by his family, wrongfully accused, and thrown into prison. In reference to Pharaoh's servants, Genesis 40:6-7 reads, "When Joseph came to them in the morning and looked at them, he saw that they were sad *and* depressed. So he asked Pharaoh's officers who were in custody with him in his master's house, 'Why do you look so dejected *and* sad today?' " Joseph was an innocent man in prison, yet he asked the king's servants why *they* were so sad. I can see Joseph going about his business completing his daily duties. He had the right attitude. He knew that God was sovereign and that God would bring him justice in due time. He didn't seem fretful at all. He was content. For sure he wanted freedom. In verse 14 he says, "But think of me when it shall be well with you and show kindness, I beg of you, to me, and mention me to Pharaoh and get me out of this house." He wanted better for himself but he was patient with God. So it is with you, be patient with God. Believe in Him and learn contentment.

You must get to the place where you are satisfied with just God. Get to the place where you are not always in search of a spouse, but you are in search of your Heavenly Father. Don't allow your desires to overtake you to the point where you don't have any peace of mind. Busy yourself in the things of God. Grow closer to the Lord. Look for ways to bless others. Become a better you. Become whole in Jesus Christ.

I urge you to meditate on the following scriptures as I have. I pray that they will bless you and that you will learn contentment in this season of your life.

Hebrews 13:5 - Keep your lives free from the love of money and be content with what you have, because God has said, "Never will I leave you; never will I forsake you."

1 Timothy 6:6-8 - But godliness with contentment is great gain. For we brought nothing into the world, and we can take nothing out of it. But if we have food and clothing, we will be content with that.

Luke 12:15 - And He said to them, "Take heed and beware of covetousness, for one's life does not consist in the abundance of the things he possesses."

1 Corinthians 7:17 - Nevertheless, people should live as a believer in whatever situation the Lord has assigned to them, just as God has called them. This is the rule I lay down in all the churches.

Matthew 6:33 - But seek (aim at and strive after) first of all His kingdom and His righteousness (His way of doing and being right), and then all these things taken together will be given you besides.

19

CONTINUE TO WAIT ON THE LORD

19

CONTINUE TO WAIT ON THE LORD

I waited patiently and expectantly for the Lord;
and He inclined to me and heard my cry.

Psalm 40:1

Although I spoke about waiting on God's timing in Chapter 2, I feel it necessary to devote an entire chapter to continuing to wait on God. It's easy to wait after you get an awesome word from God. It's easy to wait for a brief moment. But what happens when you no longer hear anything from God and you are weary from waiting? God is the same yesterday, today, and forevermore (Hebrews 13:8). As David declared in Psalm 40, he waited patiently and expectantly for the Lord. As a result, He inclined to him and heard him. As God inclined His ear to David and heard him, so He will do the same for you. Many single Christians have waited many years for God to answer their prayers for marriage. I don't claim to be a Bible scholar who knows everything about the Word of God. However, one thing that I'm sure of is that God is faithful.

If God promised, then He will make good on that promise. That one fact is what I cling to when hopelessness begins to set in my heart.

God has healed many from sickness and diseases such as cancer and sexually transmitted diseases. He alone delivered countless people from poverty, promiscuity, unhealthy relationships, a life of crime, and much more. Thus, He is still at work delivering and healing many in the Body of Christ today. If no one else knows the fiery trials that God has brought you through, you do. Why would He disregard your prayers and change His character now? If He is the same God that brought you through your many trials and healed you when the doctors said it was impossible, then He is the same God that will bless you at the appointed time with a spouse. David says, "Many, O Lord my God, are the wonderful works which You have done, and Your thoughts toward us; no one can compare with You! If I should declare and speak of them, they are too many to be numbered." (Psalm 40:5). God is always blessing us. He is always answering our prayers. He hasn't stopped. Unfortunately, some have gotten weary and stopped waiting on His promise.

Trusting God is essential to waiting on Him. Trusting Him to answer your prayer takes faith. It is by faith that God moves. For this reason I am telling you, whatever you ask for in prayer, believe (trust and be confident) that it is granted to you, and you will get it (Mark 11:24). It takes faith to wait. While you're waiting you may become weary, but the Bible tells us not to grow weary while doing good, for in due season we shall reap if we do not lose heart (Galatians 6:9). If you become weary and lose heart, you will not reap the promise. You must continue to operate in faith and wait. And this is the confidence (the assurance, the privilege of boldness) which we have in Him: [we are sure] that if we ask anything (make any request) according to His will (in agreement with His own plan), He listens to *and* hears us (1 John 5:14). If you prayed for a spouse in faith and it is according to His will, you can count it as done. For all the promises of God in Him *are* Yes, and in Him Amen, to the glory of God through us (2 Corinthians 1:20). God is telling us that the answer is yes if we are praying in faith according to His will in Jesus' name. Are you kidding me? The God of the universe promises that He will answer! This is encouraging news!

Please know that your waiting is not in vain. When God answers your prayers, it's going to blow your mind! God knows the secret desires of your heart, even the ones you don't share with others. If we delight ourselves in Him, He will bring those desires to pass (Psalm 37:4). You will be like David as he says in Psalm 40:3, "He has put a new song in my mouth, a song of praise to our God. Many shall see and fear (revere and worship) and put their trust *and* confident reliance in the Lord." Many see your waiting and many will see "The God Who Delivers" answer your prayer. Nevertheless, you must wait. Your waiting is not just about you. It's about the glory of God and how it will be revealed in your life through your faith. People that need Jesus are watching you. Those same people will see God move in your life and will turn to Jesus Christ as their Savior because you remained steadfast.

For from of old no one has heard nor perceived by the ear, nor has the eye seen a God besides You, Who works *and* shows Himself active on behalf of him who [earnestly] waits for Him (Isaiah 64:4). This is another promise from God. He acts on behalf of those who earnestly wait for Him. If you are sincerely waiting on God to answer your prayer, He will act.

You don't want to miss God and what He has for you because you allowed the enemy to discourage you. The enemy wants you to become discouraged so that you may settle with someone who God never intended for you to be with. Please don't jump ahead of God in impatience. When we're weary and discouraged we make bad choices. Get in God's presence and ask Him to strengthen you to wait. I pray that you will seek Him for strength, support, an increase in faith, answers, and everything else you need to wait.

You may be at your wit's end with waiting on God to fulfill this promise. You may be discouraged and don't want to wait any longer. Please be encouraged. You're not alone. Continue to be obedient and wait in faith. God is not the kind of God who will not bless you if you are seriously waiting on Him. He will prove His faithfulness to you in due time. You only need to continue to wait on the Lord.

20

COMMIT TO CHRIST

20

COMMIT TO CHRIST

Shadrach, Meshach and Abednego replied to him, "King Nebuchadnezzar, we do not need to defend ourselves before you in this matter. If we are thrown into the blazing furnace, the God we serve is able to deliver us from it, and he will deliver us from Your Majesty's hand. But even if he does not, we want you to know, Your Majesty, that we will not serve your gods or worship the image of gold you have set up."

Daniel 3:16-18

As single Christians, we must be committed to Christ. How can we commit to loving a person if we can't commit to loving God? I understand it's difficult to go against the grain as Christians. It's challenging to do what is right when we live in a world full of wrong. It's easier to throw in the towel and give in than it is to stand on the promises of God. The temptation to give up is everywhere. You may be doing your best to live right and wait on God.

However, every time you turn around, whether it's on television, in your own family, or friends you know, someone else is having a baby, marrying, and moving on with their lives. Meanwhile, you're still professing what God is going to do for you. As I thought about this and how I needed to commit to Christ first before committing to a man, the Lord led me to read Daniel Chapter 3.

Shadrach, Meshach and Abednego were three young men who were committed to God. They loved God with a pure love. They were about to face death, but they refused to worship any other gods. They refused to forsake their God, even in their captivity. They were confident in God enough to stand up against King Nebuchadnezzar. Shadrach, Meshach, and Abednego trusted God and remained faithful despite what everyone else was doing. Single Christians should exhibit this type of faithfulness to God, even in today's society.

The Lord showed me several things that singles in Christ can apply to their lives in the following scripture:

Then a herald cried aloud: "To you it is commanded, O peoples, nations, and languages, *that* at the time you hear the sound of the horn, flute, harp, lyre, *and* psaltery, in symphony with all kinds of music, you shall fall down and worship the gold image that King Nebuchadnezzar has set up; and whoever does not fall down and worship shall be cast immediately into the midst of a burning fiery furnace." (Daniel 3:4-5).

Whether the people believed it was right to worship this false god or not, they were doing it. Shadrach, Meshach, and Abednego on the other hand, knew who their God was. They refused to do what everyone else was doing. As you continue in your journey as a single, there will be many times when you will have to take a stand for righteousness. You will have to decide whether you will go along with the crowd or wait on God. In my own journey, there were times when I wanted to give up. There were many cold days and lonely nights where I decided I was done waiting on God. It seemed as if everyone around me was having babies and getting married. Everybody had a boyfriend or a girlfriend, even my teenage siblings! I said, "God, if you don't do something soon I'm going to ruin this testimony! I can't take this anymore!" Do you know what God did? Nothing. He did nothing and He said nothing. Therefore, I was faced with a choice: be faithful to God or walk away. Jesus says in Revelation 3:15-16, "I know your deeds, that you are neither cold nor hot. I wish you were either one or the other! So, because you are lukewarm—neither hot nor cold—I am about to spit you out of my mouth." There is no in between with God. Either you serve Him or you don't. Either you trust Him or you don't. Either you're in or you're out. There are too many Christians living lukewarm for Christ as if it's okay. As you can see in the scripture (Revelation 3:15-16), it's not okay. Decide that you will be uncompromisingly faithful to God, no matter what.

As I kept my eyes on everyone else except Jesus, it seemed as if everyone was doing whatever he or she wanted. It seemed as if everyone was living the way they wanted and I was struggling trying to live holy before God. This discouraged me many times. It made me want to do my own thing even more. Then God showed me that I should not allow the behavior of others to affect my walk with Him. The three Hebrew boys didn't care who was bowing down to worship this false god. They stood their ground, as we should. We must pray for those people that are living in disobedience and ask God to give us the strength to stand against temptation. As I read the story of Shadrach,

Meshach, and Abednego, it gave me a determination to stand for God. We must get to that place where we say, "God, I'm going to wait on you. I want to give in to temptation, but I know that you are a faithful God. I know that you have plans to prosper and not to harm me, plans to give me hope and a future." (Jeremiah 29:11). God is faithful and He rewards faithfulness. Furthermore, you never know who is watching you. Some are watching to see how you will react to your circumstances. Their deliverance could be in your faithfulness.

As you live out your life before God and people, your lifestyle may appear strange to some. A few may even belittle you for it. Some may mock and laugh. Others may believe in Jesus Christ but may not agree with your choice to live a holy life before God. Some of your friends and family may say you are "too saved" or "going too far" in your Christianity. However, the three Hebrew boys remind us of the kind of boldness that God wants us to display in Daniel 3:16, as Shadrach, Meshach, and Abednego replied, "King Nebuchadnezzar, we do not need to defend ourselves before you in this matter." You don't always need to defend yourself. God will defend you. He alone is your Rock and your

Salvation; He is your Defense *and* your Fortress, you shall not be moved (Psalm 62:6).

As Daniel Chapter 3 progresses, we see in the scripture they say to King Nebuchadnezzar, "If we are thrown into the blazing furnace, the God we serve is able to deliver us from it, and he will deliver us from Your Majesty's hand." Their confidence wasn't in what they saw with their natural eyes. Their confidence was in God. No matter what your circumstances look like, God is able to do what you ask Him to do. Be confident in God. They spoke their deliverance into the atmosphere. You need to do the same thing. You need to call those things that you want into existence (according to God's will). Speak those things that are not, as though they already are. The Bible says in Genesis 1:1-3, "In the beginning, God created the Heavens and the earth. The earth was without form and void, and darkness was over the face of the deep. And the Spirit of God was hovering over the face of the waters. And God said, 'Let there be light,' and there was light." God didn't touch anything. He spoke and so it was. We who have accepted Jesus Christ have the Spirit of God within us. If we have the Spirit of God in us, we have the same power that God has—that is to speak things into existence. Speak God's deliverance into your life.

The last part of the scripture spoke volumes to me as I read it. It reminds me that these young men were confident in whom they served. They knew God was able to deliver them, but they were so determined to do the will of God that they said, **"But even if he does not, we want you to know, Your Majesty, that we will not serve your gods or worship the image of gold you have set up"(Daniel 3:18).** Shadrach, Meshach, and Abednego were facing death but they refused to worship any other god besides the Living God. They refused to bow down and serve any other gods. This is the position we need to take, as singles, and as Christians. God is the great I AM. There is none like Him or above Him. Whether God does anything else for us, He is still God. We need to get to that place where we can truly say, "God if you never bless me with anything else I will still serve you." God was able to deliver the three Hebrew boys and He did. But they were determined in their hearts that even if God didn't deliver them, they would still serve no other god. If you believe God for a spouse and children know that God is able to do it for you. He will bless you according to His will and purpose for your life. But even if He doesn't, will you turn away and worship other gods? Will you go back into the world and do things the world's way? Will you play the harlot and cheat on God?

Ask God for the determination in your heart to serve Him all the days of your life, whether He blesses you or not. Make up your mind that you will not stop worshipping and praising Him. Set in your mind that you will continue to do the will of God even if He doesn't answer your prayers. Surely if God promised, then He will keep His promise. "God *is* not a man, that He should lie, nor a son of man, that He should repent. Has He said, and will He not do? Or has He spoken, and will He not make it good?" (Numbers 23:19).

However, God doesn't owe us anything. We owe Him everything. God is not indebted to us but we are indebted to Him. As God brought this before me, I struggled with it. I had to ask myself, "What if God never answers my prayers? Will I turn back? Will I stop serving Him? Will I go back into the world?" Then the Holy Spirit asked me, "Why do you serve God? Is it to receive something? Is it because He promised you something and you want it? Or do you serve Him from your heart?"

As I continued in my journey as a single young woman with a deep desire to be married, I endured some painful things. I can remember praying for my husband and my children. I prayed for them for years. As I continued to pray for the desires of my heart, I continued to watch as others were blessed with those very same things. As I studied the Bible certain people stuck out to me. There was one person in the Bible that I adored, so I decided to name my son after him. I went on for about four years praying for my son of that particular name, believing God for him. Most of my passwords were the name of the son I was believing God for. I would pray for him often, and at times I would be excited because I couldn't wait to meet him. Even without a spouse I believed God for this little boy. I would always pray, "Dear, Lord, don't let anybody that I know name their son after this man in the Bible. (It's not a typical biblical name). To be honest, I actually fell in love with the name. Whenever anybody would ask what I would name my children I would say, "That's between me and God." There are some secrets that I reserve for just me and God; the names of my children are one of them.

As the years went on, I continued to celebrate with others as God blessed them. One day while celebrating at a party with a close friend, she revealed not only the sex of her unborn baby, but the name. Can you guess what the name was? You got it; the very same name that I'd been praying about for the last few years of my life. Not only was I attending this party but I'd helped set up. Even after the big announcement I stayed to clean up once the party was over. As I stayed to clean up and smile for pictures, I felt like my legs were going to give out. I felt as if someone had cut my soul into a million pieces. I felt like I was going to faint. Although I was genuinely happy for her, I felt as if what I desired from God didn't matter. Here I was still waiting on God for a spouse and believing God for my son. I thought, "God, how much more will you allow me to endure? Why are you doing this? How many more of the desires of my heart will you give to others in my face?" She didn't know that I'd been praying about that name, but God knew. As I went home I couldn't even sleep that night because I couldn't understand why God would do this. It was as if my prayers for the last few years of my life were in vain.

As I prayed about it that night, the Lord reminded me of Job as he went through various trials. Job didn't do anything to deserve what

SINGLE, SAVED, & SEEKING HIM

was happening to him but God allowed it for a greater purpose. God allowed me to endure that disappointment for a greater purpose. The Lord reminded me that Job lost his actual children. I just lost a name. Although my heart was fixed on that name for years, I released that desire to God in that moment. I share that story because even in that, the enemy would try to convince me that God loved my friend more than me and that He doesn't listen to my prayers. I still don't completely understand God's reason for it but I believe that it was a test—a test of my character and my faithfulness to Him. Although I was disappointed and I cried, I set in my heart that I would serve God regardless. No matter what He didn't allow to manifest in my life and no matter what desires of my heart didn't come to pass, I was determined to love God. So I continued on in faith and in love. I'm grateful that God allowed me to face such things, as they strengthened my faith and trust in Him. Those trials also taught me how to truly love God and remain committed to Him, regardless of the circumstances.

Like Shadrach, Meshach, and Abednego, we need to commit to loving God, regardless of the hardships we face. Even if God doesn't bless you with a spouse, He is still God. Even if He

221

doesn't bless you with *every* desire of your heart, He is still God. Trust that fact. If you're going to commit to anyone, commit to Christ first. It will prove worth it in the end.

21

Be Whole in Jesus

21

BE WHOLE IN JESUS

For in Christ all the fullness of the Deity lives in bodily form, and in Christ you have been brought to fullness. He is the head over every power and authority.

Colossians 2:9-10

You are complete in Christ. You don't get your validation or wholeness from man, but from God. Everything that we need lies in Jesus. He has all power and authority. He is the Prince of Peace. Whatever you need, He has it. Do you need emotional healing, a boost of self-esteem, or freedom from your anxieties? Turn to Him. Every insecurity that you have, bring it to Jesus before you think about unloading it on another person. As people, we are only equipped to handle a certain amount from other people. Only God can handle the deep hidden things. For example, if you have insecurity issues, whether it's from an incident you experienced as a child or because of a past relationship, you must allow

God to heal that area before you marry. If God so wills, He will provide you with a partner that is equipped with the grace to handle it. However, why would you want to dump that much responsibility on another person? Many times, we turn to people as void-fillers when we should be turning to Jesus. At times God will separate you from others just to have you to Himself. Healing, restoration, and revival takes place in His presence. That's what He wants to do for you in this season. Unfortunately, some of us would rather spend time with a man or a woman than spend time in God's holy presence. Some of us need healing and restoration in our minds and in our emotions. You may have some strongholds that God wants to break before He sends that person into your life.

Don't shun this time alone with God. It's for a purpose. Some people don't want to face the fact that they have issues that need to be resolved. They'd rather cover it up with a new relationship, which will only make the scars deeper. Begin to ask the Lord what's in you that He wants to take out. Ask Him what He wants to work on in you. In doing this, you must be honest with yourself. You know more than anyone else does what your issues are. Only God can resolve those issues, not the arms of another lover. Some people need mental stability. There is nothing wrong with going to a psychologist to talk to about your issues. Many people are deeply disturbed in their minds and emotions from past relationships. You can't lug around old baggage and ask God for a spouse, with no intention of unloading that old baggage first. All you will do is bring that old baggage to the new situation. Also, if you are still carrying around a torch for an old flame, you might as well stop looking. You must get over the last relationship. If not, it will be unhealthy for you and the new person. If you still have someone from your past in your heart, how can you have room for the one God is going to send? I prayed all the time that God would heal me from my past relationships and remove them from my heart. I don't want my future husband to have to compete with anyone else for my love. I want him to have all of my heart, not some of it. I wouldn't want to marry someone who still has feelings for an ex and emotional baggage from their past relationship. So why would I expect someone else to do it? How can God send you a mate when you have people from your past in your heart? There won't be enough room for that person if you don't allow yourself the healing you need right now.

Marrying before you acknowledge or
embrace your completeness in Christ can cause
major problems in a marriage. If you are waiting
on someone else to make you whole or validate
you, you will be disappointed. I believe marriage
is two people who are whole in Christ coming
together to exemplify Christ's love relationship
with the church. If you feel incomplete, then
there is an area in you that you have not allowed
Christ to fill. You may have a desire that is
unfulfilled, yet you should not feel unfulfilled.
Your purpose is fulfilled in Christ. He is the One
who makes you complete, lacking nothing.
David said in Psalm 23, "The LORD is my
shepherd, I shall not want." He is saying, "I lack
nothing. I have everything that I need. I am
whole and well taken care of in Him." It didn't
matter what his situation was; David knew in
Him, he was complete.

Let's examine Colossians 2:9-10, the
amplified version, as it states, **"For in Him the
whole fullness of Deity (the Godhead)
continues to dwell in bodily form [giving
complete expression of the divine nature].
And you are in Him, made full *and* having
come to fullness of life [in Christ you too are
filled with the Godhead—Father, Son and
Holy Spirit—and reach full spiritual stature].**

And He is the Head of all rule and authority [of every angelic principality and power]." Jesus is complete. In Him the whole fullness of the Holy Trinity dwells. The divine nature of God rests in Jesus, even when He walked the earth. God lacks nothing. He needs nothing. If this is the nature of Jesus and you are in Him, then you have this same nature. You lack nothing. You need nothing. You are filled with the Godhead—Father, Son, and Holy Spirit. He's in you. Therefore, you don't need another person to make you complete because you're already complete in Him.

Know that God loves you and wants to heal every part of you. You are whole and complete in Jesus Christ. Be whole in the name of Jesus. I pray that you will meditate on the following scriptures:

Ephesians 3:19 - [That you may really come] to know [practically, through experience for yourselves] the love of Christ, which far surpasses mere knowledge [without experience]; that you may be filled [through all your being] unto all the fullness of God [may have the richest measure of the divine Presence, and become a body wholly filled and flooded with God Himself]!

Philippians 4:19 - And my God will liberally supply (fill to the full) your every need according to His riches in glory in Christ Jesus.

1 Timothy 1:14 - And the grace (unmerited favor and blessing) of our Lord [actually] flowed out superabundantly and beyond measure for me, accompanied by faith and love that are [to be realized] in Christ Jesus.

Remember to love yourself. If you don't know how to love God or yourself, how can you love another person? If you don't know God, you don't know what real love is. **He who does not love has not become acquainted with God [does not and never did know Him], for God is love (1 John 4:8).**

Concentrate on loving God and loving yourself. Always know that you have His Spirit in you. Therefore, be whole in Jesus' name!

22

PREPARE YOURSELF FOR MARRIAGE

PREPARE YOURSELF FOR MARRIAGE

[Put first things first.] Prepare your work outside and get it ready for yourself in the field; and afterward build your house and establish a home.

Proverbs 24:27

God desires for us to use wisdom. Therefore, we should prepare ourselves for marriage in the same way we prepare for anything else. Before you make any major decisions in your life, you need to seek God and prepare first. God uses preparation and processing many times in the Bible. If you notice, some of the "greats" that God used went through a season of preparation and processing. The worst thing you can do is enter into a marriage unprepared. Some spend all their time preparing for the marriage spiritually (prayer, fasting, etc.) and fail to prepare for the marriage in the natural, although both are important. Jesus says, "Suppose one of you wants to build a tower. Won't you first sit down and estimate the cost to see if you have enough money to complete it? For if you lay the foundation and are not able to finish it, everyone who sees it will ridicule you, saying, 'This person began to build and wasn't able to finish'." (Luke 14:28-30). I was guilty of this. We need to prepare now so we are not caught off guard when it does happen.

While you are single, there are a few things you can learn before entering into this next chapter of your life. While you have the time, develop yourself spiritually, emotionally, mentally, and financially.

SPIRITUAL PREPARATION

There is plenty you can do to prepare yourself spiritually to be a godly spouse. Praying, fasting, and meditating in God's presence are some things you can do to prepare.

Prayer is one of the most important practices you can do in this season. It is through communication with God that we learn to hear His voice, take counsel, and instruction. Communicating with God about your desire is not good enough. You need to seek God about the things in you that He desires to perfect. Sometimes, God will delay a promise because there are things in us that we cannot take into the "Promise Land." For instance, if you are selfish, short-tempered, impatient, or easily discouraged, you may want to hold off on becoming joined to another person. You may want to allow God to perfect you in those areas first. Let me explain. Whomever you marry is an imperfect human being. They are imperfect just like you. Therefore, patience is needed. Moreover, life will continue to happen. There will be difficulties. You can't become easily discouraged when bad times come and quit on your partner. So, ask God to reveal your weak areas so that He can strengthen them. It's in prayer and our current circumstances that God will reveal the hidden and "not so nice" things about us. When He reveals these things, we must be receptive and willing to change. Ask Him to show you how to pray for your future spouse. God is preparing you both in this season. You're not the only one who needs prayer right now. There may be areas in their life that God wants to perfect. Intercede on their behalf in this season.

In addition, pray that God will prepare you regarding spiritual matters. Please don't think that once you get married you won't have to pray as much. A married friend of mine once told me, "You think that you pray a lot now? Ha, just wait until you get married!" Gird yourself with the Word of God. This is a good time to allow God to develop you. Learn how to apply the Word of God to your life, pray in the Spirit, and seek God in His Word and in prayer. Your spouse and children will need you to intercede for them. Do you think the enemy will slack off in his attacks because you get married? He will come even harder because he hates unity. Learn how to fight in the Spirit. There may be nights when you have to pray in the midnight hour for your spouse. Get into the habit of being in the presence of the Lord. Petition with God now on behalf of your spouse and children. Don't wait; be prepared.

Learn how to enter into His presence for all that you need. Don't wait until you're in a relationship to learn to turn to God. Do it now. You need to know that God is your Provider for everything.

Genesis 22:14 - Abraham called the name of that place Jehovah-Jireh, the LORD is my provider. As it is said to this day, "In the LORD's mountain it will be provided."

A man can receive nothing, unless it has been given to him from Heaven (John 3:27). Everything you receive is from God above. He is your Source. Everything and everyone is a resource. He provides strength, wisdom, insight, encouragement, and help in the time of trouble. He may use your family, friends, job, or spouse as a resource. However, God is your only Source. I can remember times when I was discouraged about waiting on God for my spouse. Some of my friends and even my pastors would speak a word of encouragement at just the right time. I know that God put it in their hearts to do so. They were the resource, but God was the Source. Even when you are married, there will be times too hard and issues too deep for your spouse to absorb. Those are reserved for the Lord. Remember: the Lord is your portion (Psalms 119:57) and your exceedingly great reward (Genesis 15:1).

FINANCIAL PREPARATION

1 Corinthians 4:2 says, "Moreover, it is [essentially] required of stewards that a man should be found faithful [proving himself worthy of trust]." Can God trust you with your finances right now? Are you faithful in your tithes and

offerings? Do you pay your bills on time? Do you squander all your money on unnecessary things? Do you pay what you owe or allow the bill collectors to keep calling with no intention to pay? The Bible says in Psalm 37:21, "The wicked borrows and does not repay, but the righteous shows mercy and gives." When you get married, your money is no longer just your money. You will share it with your other half and you will share responsibilities with your other half. Singles should take this alone time to allow God to show you how to become a good steward. Your spouse will need to know that they can trust you with the finances. You will need to be a trustworthy spouse, even in financial matters. Learn how to budget, save, and spend wisely.

1 Timothy 5:8 says, "If anyone fails to provide for his relatives, and especially for those of his own family, he has disowned the faith [by failing to accompany it with fruits] and is worse than an unbeliever [who performs his obligation in these matters]." You must be able to take care of your family. God needs to be able to trust you with the spouse for which you are praying. Luke 16:10 says, "He who is faithful in a very little [thing] is faithful also in much, and he who is dishonest *and* unjust in a very little [thing] is

dishonest *and* unjust also in much (Luke 16:10)."
If you're unfaithful in the little things now, how
can God trust you with the big things later (i.e. a
spouse, a household, a godly marriage?)

I remember a few years back, I was
sitting in my car on my lunch break having one
of my talks with God. I asked, "God, what's
going on? What's the problem?" The Holy Spirit
led me to Genesis 2:18, Now the Lord God said,
"It is not good (sufficient, satisfactory) that the
man should be alone; I will make him a helper
(suitable, adapted, complementary) for him."
(Genesis 2:18). Adam was alone (not lonely). He
needed a helpmate. Therefore, God provided for
him a wife. The word that God showed me was
make. God said He would **make** him a helper. I
realized then that God was preparing me. He was
fashioning me to be the helpmate that my future
husband would need. God is preparing you for
your marriage. Allow the Holy Spirit to do the
work so you'll be ready when the time comes.
He won't allow you to come into one of His
children's lives just any old way. There must be
preparation. When the appointed time comes,
God is not going to send you just anybody. He is
going to send you a person that He has fashioned
just for you. As I think of preparation, I think of
Esther as she prepared to meet with King

Ahasuerus. She wasn't thrust into his presence. Preparation was required. It took a whole year of preparation before any one of the maidens could come into King Ahasuerus' presence.

Now when the turn of each maiden came to go in to King Ahasuerus, after the regulations for the women had been carried out for twelve months—since this was the regular period for their beauty treatments, six months with oil of myrrh and six months with sweet spices *and* perfumes and the things for the purifying of the women (Esther 2:12).

Don't despise this season, God is purifying and preparing you. As He is preparing you, you are being purified from the mindsets and ways of the world. You are being cleansed from the stains that past hurts have left on your soul. Allow God to prepare you in this time.

23

PURPOSE IN THIS SEASON

23

PURPOSE IN THIS SEASON

To everything there is a season, and a time for
every matter or purpose under Heaven.

Ecclesiastes 3:1

Many Christians don't understand the
concept of seasons. We need to fully understand
seed and harvest time. Every chapter of your life
is a season. You will enter many different
seasons in your lifetime. No matter what you do,
or what you say, your seasons must change.
They will change according to God's perfect will
and plan for your life. When God promises us
something like a spouse, He may not release that
promise for years. He will not release it until the
appointed time. In the meantime, you must
understand the season that you are currently
operating in so you can be fruitful in it. God is
not a wasteful God. Why would He have you in
a season, regardless of what the season is, for no
apparent reason at all? There is something that
God desires from you in this time of your life.

Yes, I know you want to get married, but that's a different season. You're not in that season right now. There is a purpose for **this** season of your life. There is a reason why you are not married yet. God wants to fulfill one of His purposes for you in the earth in this time. However, you will only know that purpose by seeking God.

Ecclesiastes 3:1 says, "To everything there is a season." Your single status is a season and there is a purpose for it. As you seek God about your marital status, be sure to seek God about your purpose in this season of your life. Many people miss God or what God wants to do in their lives because they are out of season. They become so hasty to get married that they fail to accomplish what God desires for them to accomplish while they are single. If God wanted you married, you would be. The key is to find out what God wants you to birth in this season. For many, God has placed desires, accomplishments, and goals inside of you. For others God wants to heal you as past relationships have left you scarred and bruised. God wants to give some people back their joy as the enemy has stripped them of it in the past. For some this is a time for preparation before you get married. Therefore, there is a reason for this time. You must seek God to find out what it is.

At first I couldn't care less about a season or timing. I wanted my husband and that was the end of the story. However, as I sought God more, I began to understand that my life, even after I'm married, will consist of many accomplishments and assignments for God. I began to understand that I am a vessel used by God to accomplish His will in the earth. There is more to me than my marital status. There is more to you than your marital status. God is always working. We should always be working alongside Him. Seek God about those desires that He's placed inside of you. The ministry that He is pressing on your heart: why haven't you gotten started? The book that is burning a hole in your soul because it has yet to be written: why haven't you written it? The business ideas and college degree you said you were going to complete: what happened? I hope you're not waiting for a spouse to come into your life so you can be happy and then accomplish your goals. If so you can forget about it. Many times God will not release your blessing until you have been obedient to what He's called you to do first.

God wants you to use this time wisely. The Bible tells us to walk circumspectly, not as fools but as wise, redeeming time, because the days are evil. Therefore do not be unwise, but understand what the will of the Lord is (Ephesians 5:15-17). We're supposed to make the most of every opportunity. You should make the most of this time in your life. As Ecclesiastes Chapter 3 goes on, it gives different examples of times and the purposes for them:

A time to be born, and a time to die; a time to plant, and a time to pluck up what is planted; a time to kill, and a time to heal; a time to break down, and a time to build up; a time to weep, and a time to laugh; a time to mourn, and a time to dance; a time to cast away stones, and a time to gather stones together; a time to embrace, and a time to refrain from embracing; a time to seek, and a time to lose; a time to keep, and a time to cast away; a time to tear, and a time to sew; a time to keep silence, and a time to speak; a time to love, and a time to hate; a time for war, and a time for peace (Ecclesiastes 3:2-8).

As you can see, there is a time for everything. There is a right and wrong time for everything. When you get married, it will be the right time for that. Right now is the time for something else. Right now is the time for God to mature you. It's the time for God to show Himself strong on your behalf. This is the time to

SINGLE, SAVED, & SEEKING HIM

get to know God personally. Psalm 103:7 says, "He made known His ways to Moses, His acts to the children of Israel." The children of Israel knew God's works. They saw the miracles and great things He did for them, but they didn't know Him intimately. God wants to be intimate with you in this season. Exodus 33:11 says, "So the LORD spoke to Moses face to face, as a man speaks to his friend." God wants to speak with you as you speak to your friends. This is the time to get to know God like never before. As you draw closer to God in this season, He will draw closer to you (James 4:8). God will then begin to give you the desires of your heart. He will begin to fill your heart with those desires that He has in mind for you to accomplish. He will begin to restore your mind and heal you of things past.

To become fruitful in this season, you must understand the purpose of your current season. You must have understanding of the signs of the current time and what you are to do. The Bible mentions men from Issachar who came to assist David in battle as he was to become the next king of Israel. They were men who understood the times and knew what Israel should do (1 Chronicles 12:32). These men had wisdom and understanding to assess the times. They analyzed the situation so they would know the right thing to do. They operated in wisdom and understanding as we need to do in this season. God doesn't want you wasting your time trying to find a new date. God has invested His time, gifts, and talents in you. Your time, gifts, and talents are not to be wasted in this season as you believe God for a spouse. The spouse will come as you believe God for that person. However, God wants you fruitful now, in this season. He's given your life purpose now. You don't get purpose when you get married. God has preordained your purpose. You have purpose now! You are God's handiwork, created in Christ Jesus to do good works, which God prepared in advance for you to do (Ephesians 2:10). Therefore, you already have purpose in Christ. There is purpose in this season for your life. Fulfill your purpose.

24

ENJOY YOUR LIFE

24

ENJOY YOUR LIFE

The thief does not come except to steal, and to kill, and to destroy. I have come that they may have life, and that they may have it more abundantly.

John 10:10

Jesus came and laid down His life so that we may have life and have it more abundantly. He said the thief comes to steal, kill, and destroy (John 10:10). The feelings of low self-esteem, depression, and the wilderness mentality of "I'll be happy when..." are from the enemy. He wants to steal your joy, kill your zeal for God, and destroy your life. He'll feed you lies to discourage you. He'll try to deceive you to think that you are missing out on all that God has for you because you are still single. Jesus came that you may have life. The Bible doesn't say, "...that you may have life when you get married." He wants you to live your life now! He said that He came that we may have life more abundantly. The word abundant means rich, sufficient, lavish, bountiful, full, and overflowing. He came that your life may be rich, sufficient (lacking nothing), bountiful, and full. He wants you to a have an abundant life, now! Jesus didn't lay down His life for you to wait until you're married to have a good life. In John 10:10, Jesus used the word "may" twice. I wondered why he used "may" instead of "will" in the scripture. I believe it's because many singles don't choose the abundant life, they choose the opposite. I was this way for a long time. I thought, "I'll enjoy my life even more when I get married. It will be better then." Sometimes I would allow myself to become depressed about my marital status instead of enjoying the free time that God allowed me to share with Him.

It's a choice to enjoy your life. When those negative feelings and thoughts come, shake them off and speak life into your situation. Get up and enjoy your life. Time is one of the most precious gifts that God has given us. Once it's gone, it doesn't come back. He is able to redeem your time, but the hours and days you wasted, they're gone forever. You will never get the time back that you wasted being frustrated and depressed about your marital status. God doesn't want you wasting the time He gave you on that.

Jesus said, "Come to Me, all *you* who labor and are heavy laden, and I will give you rest. Take My yoke upon you and learn from Me, for I am gentle and lowly in heart, and you will find rest for your souls. For My yoke *is* easy and My burden is light." Some people choose to carry the weight of the world on their shoulders. He wants you to lay your burdens down and enjoy your life. He wants you to cast all your care upon Him, because He cares for you (1 Peter 5:7). He doesn't want you to worry about whom or when it's going to happen. Cast those cares on Him. Jesus told His disciples, "Let not your heart be troubled; you believe in God, believe also in Me." (John 14:1). Don't trouble yourself with the "what ifs" of the situation. Trust God enough to let him handle the specifics and enjoy your life.

King Solomon said, "I know that there is nothing better for them than to be glad and to get *and* do good as long as they live; And also that every man should eat and drink and enjoy the good of all his labor—it is the gift of God." (Ecclesiastes 3:12-13). Your life, your friends, your work, and your family are all gifts from God. You should enjoy them. Life is for the living. This is the time for you to travel, see places you've never seen, and go places you've never gone. Take a spa day to relax or read your favorite book in the park on a beautiful day. Take chances and meet new people. Live your life.

I know that whatever God does, it endures forever; nothing can be added to it nor anything taken from it. God does it so that men will [reverently] fear Him [revere and worship Him, knowing that He is] (Ecclesiastes 3:14). Since everything God does endures forever and nothing can be added or taken away from it, why worry about it? God is in control of your life. He is sovereign. His judgments stand forever. That which is has already been, and what is to be has already been; and God requires an account of what is past (Ecclesiastes 3:15). Whatever God is going to do is already done. So why worry yourself? Live your life to the fullest now. You don't have to wait until another person comes into your life to be happy. Enjoy those people that God has placed in your life in this season. Live…and enjoy your life.

CONCLUSION: BE ENCOURAGED!

CONCLUSION: BE ENCOURAGED!

Living single and saved is not easy at all. Particularly when you have believed God for a spouse for what seems an eternity. The nights you spend alone yearning for someone to hold become a nuisance. Wondering if you will ever have children if you don't already is upsetting. If being single is not what you want, it can be painful at times.

On the other hand, there is an upside to being single. The ability to move when and how you want is a blessing. We who are single, have the freedom to serve Christ at a capacity that married people can't. Paul says in 1 Corinthians 7:32-33 that, "He who is unmarried cares for the things of the Lord—how he may please the Lord. But he who is married cares about the things of the world—how he may please *his* wife." He also says, "The unmarried woman cares about the things of the Lord, that she may be holy both in body and in spirit. But she who is married cares about the things of the world—how she may please *her* husband." Earlier in the chapter he says, each person has his own gift from God in terms of singleness or marriage (1 Corinthians 7:7-8). Being a single person in Christ can be a gift, depending on your perspective. You can choose to devote your time to the needs of others in the Body of Christ. You can use this time to become all that God has destined for you to become. This is the time to start that business, finish school, travel the world, write that book, and develop a deeper relationship with Christ. Then again, you can use this time to become depressed, complain, have pity parties, envy others, or just give up. The choice is yours.

I'm not saying this journey is an effortless one, by any means. It's far from that. Many times, I have become weary and tempted to go my own way. The truth is, I know that God's will is better than my way. I know I will miss God if I turn away. Don't miss God because you are weary. Sometimes it seems as if God doesn't care about how we feel as singles. The truth is He does care. He who planted the ear, shall He not hear? He who formed the eye, shall He not see? (Psalm 94:9) He hears your prayers and sees your hardships.

God will hear and bless you. However, many of us need to become whole in Jesus Christ before we can become one with another person. How do we become whole in Jesus Christ? By seeking the Face of God. By allowing Him to transform us from the inside out. By giving God complete control so that His perfect will may be done in and through us.

As a single person, you must know that you have purpose. You have value and you are not forgotten. God says in Deuteronomy 31:8, "And the LORD, He *is* the One who goes before you. He will be with you; He will not leave you nor forsake you; do not fear nor be dismayed." You are not alone because you don't have a spouse. God is with you. At times, it may seem as if no one understands or even cares about the battles you face every day. Be encouraged because you are not alone. People may not see the tears you cry out of loneliness and frustration, but God sees. I know it sounds cliché but God will not put more on you than you can bear. He knows what you can handle. He knows all things. We have to learn to submit our will in exchange for His. *He who loves his life will lose it, and he who hates his life in this world will keep it for eternal life* (John 12:25). The problem arises when we want our own will more than we want the will of God. You are single for such a time as this. Although it may not be favorable, it is God's will for your life right now. The more you wrestle with God about this, the more frustrated you will become.

Trust God and His timing in this season. Be whole in Jesus Christ. Allow the presence and love of God to overtake you in prayer and worship. Cling to the Word of God. Speak life and the Word of God into your circumstances. Commit to loving God with your whole heart. Seek Him for your purpose. Become greater in this time of your life. Be encouraged, you are not alone. I pray that you are inspired and strengthened to continue in Jesus Christ and to continue believing God for your miracle.

Be blessed.

A SINGLE SACRIFICE

It's a sacrifice to live this way
To obey Your Word
Despite what scoffers may say
To keep my body
Which longs for another body
To keep my mind
Although I feel forgotten at times
An exchange of Your desires for mine
To have faith for Your promises in Your time
The lonely mornings and cold nights
I offer them to You as I remember Your sacrifice
The shame You bore as You hung on the cross
The shame I feel when the "You're not married
yet?" questions are tossed
Chosen for this fight
To be obedient
To be a living sacrifice
To study Your Word and preach the Gospel
To remain in You
Although the world tells me not to
Pour out Your Spirit upon me
To help me live this life
As I offer to You a single sacrifice

A.M.

ABOUT THE AUTHOR

Born and raised in Newark, NJ, Amina relocated to Philadelphia, PA in 2009 as she answered the call of God for a new life in Christ. She is now a member at Brand New Life Christian Center in Philadelphia where she serves as the Singles Ministry Leader for young adults. An aspiring writer since an adolescent, Amina has fulfilled her lifelong dream of becoming a published author through Words From Heaven Publishing where she is the founder and CEO. She also maintains *Words by Amina*, which is a faith-based blog purposed to address the topics that Christians face in their daily lives. In an effort to perfect her craft, she is currently pursuing a Master of Fine Arts degree in English and Creative Writing at Southern New Hampshire University. As a writer, blogger, and poet, her desire is to encourage the hearts of God's people through her experiences and the Word of God.

You may visit Amina's blog at:
www.aminaswords.blogspot.com

To contact the author please write to:

Words From Heaven Publishing

P.O. Box 44473

Philadelphia, PA 19144

Or log on to www.wfhpublishing.com